PROVINCETOWN PAINTERS
1890's–1970's

**EVERSON MUSEUM OF ART
SYRACUSE, NEW YORK**

Edited and Foreword by
Ronald A. Kuchta

Text by Dorothy Gees Seckler

CONTENTS

7   **FOREWORD** *by Ronald A. Kuchta*

11   **ACKNOWLEDGEMENTS**

13   **HISTORY OF THE PROVINCETOWN ART COLONY**
       by Dorothy Gees Seckler

107   **NOTES ON OTHER EUROPEAN AND AMERICAN ARTISTS' COLONIES**

113   **ILLUSTRATIONS**

271   **BIBLIOGRAPHY**

278   **APPENDIX**

288   **LENDERS**

291   **EVERSON MUSEUM OF ART BOARD OF TRUSTEES AND STAFF**

FOREWORD

Artists, especially painters and writers have a great advantage over most of us who work, in that they can more easily choose the location for their work and can if they like move from place to place, seasonally or however often they prefer or can afford. Their materials and products are easily portable and they don't necessarily have to be close to their markets continuously. Even though most successful artists gravitate to marketing centers such as New York, Los Angeles, or London, they don't necessarily have to live in these cities all of the time. Beautiful natural places, such as Cape Cod, Long Island, the Coast of Maine, the Catskills, the Monterey Peninsula and the mountains of New Mexico in America have thus become chosen places for painters and writers. Whether they are successful or not, they have the satisfaction of spending their lives in environments that are aesthetically chosen — chosen with the same faculty which is the means of their very metier.

The idea for this exhibition came therefore partly from my envy and admiration for the many artists who have had the good fortune to have lived and worked in one of those chosen places — Provincetown.

Provincetown Painters concerns itself with painters who have painted in Provincetown, Massachusetts, America's most prolific art colony, or who used it as subject matter, or who were inspired or seduced in some way by its locale.

Provincetown on Cape Cod has long been recognized as a unique place in terms of its geography, as well as in terms of its inhabitants. The most unusual aspect of its history is the fact that it has attracted a phenomenal number of artists within the past eighty years. Perhaps only Greenwich Village in the nation's largest city has been more densely populated by artists and their followers who gather to enjoy the milieu of art. Provincetown, with a steady permanent population of about 3,500 over the past 75 years, has seen hundreds of artists migrate to it seasonally as well as year-round. Neither Woodstock, New York; Easthampton, New York; New Hope, Pennsylvania; Taos, New Mexico; Old Lyme, Connecticut; Ogunquit, Maine; nor Carmel, California can match in reputation the tradition of Provincetown as a place that has produced American art. Few musuems with comprehensive collections of American art are without some paintings painted in Provincetown (the Everson has forty-seven, Syracuse University Collection has over twenty). Provincetown is the origin of many paintings famous in the history of twentieth-century American art, not only the place where they were painted, but where they were first exhibited, discussed and sold. Along with its many artists, the town has supported art schools, art clubs, museums, galleries, frame shops and art supply stores, the number and quality of which have hardly been matched in many major cities.

Why this phenomenon? What attracted so many artists to Provincetown — an extremity on the map of the country pointing east? Perhaps its remoteness and perhaps Nature most of all, appealing to realists, impressionists, expressionists and abstractionists alike. As an historic old fishing village at the end of a long peninsula surrounded by blue sea and a wild desert-like landscape of dunes, it offered brilliant light, fresh air and the drama of weather and sea. It especially appealed to the romantic nature and free spirit of artists. Added to its natural appeal were its people. Provincetown has always been a casual place with few pretensions. It was never a resort for the merely rich or fashionable. Life-style for townspeople and artists alike tended toward simplicity. So, as nature dominated the environment of Provincetown, artists passing through in cycles somehow saturated the atmosphere of the small town as well. This is not to suggest that Provincetown is or always has been an idyllic place. As it has been a retreat for many, some individuals there have always seemed to have their backs up against the wall. As an intense, compact, small town it's had its share of small-town mindedness too. Prejudice, greed, contentiousness and division are sometimes all the more apparent there because of its small size and because of the vocal nature of its democratic citizens. In addition to these chronic conditions, every so often an element of tragedy — a murder, a fire, a sunken ship, touches the lives of everyone in the community.

Young painters have come to Provincetown continually since the 1890s to seek teachers in the summer, such as Charles Hawthorne, George Elmer Browne, Ambrose Webster, Henry Hensche, Karl Knaths, Edwin Dickinson, Hans Hofmann, Leo Manso, Victor Candell and Morris Davidson. It has always been a good place to learn and to experiment because of its tolerant and cosmopolitan make-up. (When a less romantic, less-nature oriented, more urban art came into vogue in the late sixties, some painters seemed to prefer the city and the slickness of more affluent resorts for their recreation.)

The exhibition pays tribute to Provincetown on its 250th anniversary as a town (it was incorporated in 1777, before which it was a part of Truro, its immediate neighbor to the south, today a much smaller community). *Provincetown Painters* consists of the works of many artists; some nationally known (Charles Hawthorne, Milton Avery, Marsden Hartley, Charles Demuth, Stuart Davis, Childe Hassam, Ernest Lawson, Ben Shahn, Raphael Soyer, Niles Spencer, William Zorach, Frederick Waugh, Chaim Gross, Karl Knaths, Edwin Dickenson, Hans Hofmann, Robert Motherwell, Adolph Gottlieb, Franz Kline, Red Grooms, etc.); others best-known locally, who may deserve to be better known (Ambrose Webster, Mary Cecil Allen, Gerrit Beneker, Oliver Chaffee, Reeves Euler, Henry Hensche, Charles Heinz, Bruce McKain, Phil Malicoat, Blanche Lazzell, Gerrit Hondius, William Freed, Lilian Orlowsky, Nanno De Groot, Arthur Cohen, etc.); and a few anonymous ship painters completely unknown. Some of these artists have spent only a few summers in Provincetown (Childe Hassam, Marsden Hartley, Jackson Pollock, Lee Krasner, etc.). Others have spent their entire mature lives, summer and winter, in Provincetown (Henry Hensche, Karl Knaths, Bruce McKain, Phil Malicoat, Reeves Euler, Jim Forsberg, Sal Del Deo, Myron Stout, etc.). Some spent practically all their summers for many years in the Provincetown area (Charles Hawthorne, Edward Hopper, Frederick Waugh, Hans Hofmann, Robert Motherwell, Jack Tworkov, William Freed, Lila Katzen, Alvin Ross, Fritz Bultman, etc.). And artists came and settled from all over America, Europe and Japan (Reeves Euler from Nevada, Edward Corbett from California, Bruce McKain from Indiana, Fritz Bultman from Louisiana, Nanno De Groot from Holland, Hans Hofmann from Germany, Xavier Gonzalez from Spain, Taro Yamamoto from Japan, Peter Hutchinson from England, Nassos Daphnis from Greece).

Within the realm of *Provincetown Painters* have been included artists who have lived and worked on its outskirts in neighboring Truro and Wellfleet, since these artists (Ben Shahn, Edward Hopper, Xavier Gonzalez, Jerry Farnsworth, Helen Sawyer, etc.) usually found their social life and exhibited in Provincetown. To the extent possible, paintings have been chosen which have actually been painted at or inspired by the Outer Cape. Occasionally that data was impossible to determine and in some cases the paintings sought were unavailable. Certainly all the painters who ever painted in Provincetown are not included, although the exhibition is basically inclusive rather than exclusive, as it attempts to show the range and to survey the periods of painting there. As many painters as I have been able to determine as having lived and worked in Provincetown between 1890 and 1970 are included in an appendix to this book.

As interest in American art deepens, as America becomes both more mature and more decentralized culturally, and as the idea of the great city as a monolith of art and culture erodes, it seems more and more appropriate to explore such places as Provincetown, a place in which so much painting has been produced.

While no "Provincetown School" is exactly posited, certainly not one to compete with the Boston School or the New York School, the fact is that many of the artists associated with both these schools of painting did much of their work in Provincetown. Not so much a cultural center, however, Provincetown has proved to be a good working place for artists. Something about the intense sunlight reflected off the sea and dunes for the impressionists; the fraternity of artists and "picturesque" subject matter for the realists; the energy of nature and existential apartness for the abstract expressionists, seemingly had much to do with their vitality in this venerable New England town. Nature coupled with a tolerant, modest, nature-tested year-round population of Portuguese, Yankee and bohemian townspeople has made Provincetown more than the fishing village it had been the first hundred and fifty years of its existence. Its nature, ecological and human, made it a working place and an ideal resort for painters and writers alike (among the best known writers on the Outer Cape have been Eugene O'Neil, John Dos Passos, George Santayana, Edmund Wilson, e.e. cummings, Tennessee Williams and Norman Mailer).

The intent of this exhibition is to convey a sense of the history of Provincetown the "art colony," and to demonstrate the creativity as well as the great productivity of the painters which its environment has inspired.

Ronald A. Kuchta

ACKNOWLEDGEMENTS

In organizing this exhibition and catalogue the assistance of many individuals has been of great value of course. Some provided information, others transportation, others research, others opinions and suggestions, others accommodations, still others labor and clerical work. I will not sort them all out here, but will list my helpers together since without any of these devoted friends and aids the completion of this ambitious project would obviously not have been possible. My deepest appreciation to the following for their collaboration and cooperation in the organization of *Provincetown Painters:* Michael Pommier, Yeffe Kimball, Josephine Del Deo, Ray Martin Wells, Molly Malone Cook, Mary Oliver, Elizabeth Zogbaum, Nathan Halper, Sandra Levin, Ciro Cozzi, Geraldine Ramer, Margaret Mayo, Mrs. Daniel C. Merrill, Hazel Hawthorne Warner, George Wilford Grozier, Josiah Child, The Provincetown Advocate, Ami Belsky, Marie Culver, Suzanne Evans, Marina Lary, Ruth Stainton, Peg Weiss, Philip Van Lengen, Pat Hill, Elaine Mazur, Barbara Knowlton, Anthony Murrell, John Hood and Gussie Will Alex.

Finding someone to undertake the writing of a brief history of this popular art colony where so many artists, as well as writers, had thrived, would not seem to be a very difficult task. Yet, compiling necessary information and attempting to write an evenhanded chronicle within the time allotted (a year and a half) proved formidable. Dorothy Gees Seckler was a logical choice for this project. She was suggested to me by my photographer, literary agent friend, Molly Malone Cook, whose own acquaintance with the present colony of writers is intimate. Dorothy is a journalist, painter, and devoted summer art colonist whose personal knowledge and friendship with many of the artists of Provincetown over the past three decades has been extensive. Before obtaining a degree at Columbia, Dorothy Gees Seckler was graduated from the Maryland Institute College of Arts and was awarded a traveling scholarship on which she studied independently in Europe. While she was Associate Editor of Art News Magazine, she received the American Federation of Arts Award for outstanding writing in the field of American Art (1952). As contributing editor of Art in America for more than a decade, she wrote cover stories on, among others, Robert Rauschenberg and Louise Nevelson, as well as such widely quoted features as *A Folklore of the Banal* and *The Audience is the Medium.* She was a lecturer on the history of art and contemporary art at New York University, The City College of New York and Pratt Institute and is a contributor to the McGraw Hill Encyclopedia of World Art.

She has bravely set forth the story of Provincetown as an "insider" and practically as the recipient of an "oral tradition" (much of her information was recalled from tapes she made in the sixties while documenting artists for the Archives of American Art) since so little had been chronologically transcribed before. We therefore have in her essay a definitive preliminary history, rich with personal reflections and interesting anecdotes only a firsthand reporter could possibly convey.

My thanks also to Henry Hensche and to Walter P. Chrysler, Jr., without whose encouragement and sustained acquaintance, I would not have been so thoroughly introduced to the art and artists of Provincetown seventeen years ago.

Provincetown Painters is made possible through a grant from the National Endowment for the Arts, a Federal Agency and the New York State Council on the Arts.

Ronald A. Kuchta
April, 1977

A HISTORY OF THE PROVINCETOWN ART COLONY

Introduction

The clear, concise and very comforting confines required by exacting scholarship in any field were never established in writing the story of the Provincetown Art Colony. With its countless artists, feuding coteries, rapid shifts of reigning styles, with its burgeoning schools, active Art Association and provocative personalities, the Colony has provided a narrative which has constantly expanded and spilled over intended boundaries in a rich, colorful and untidy torrent of data. Looking back I can reflect ruefully that a fool rushed in where experts feared to tread, yet at the time it seemed not only to me but also to Ronald A. Kuchta of the Everson Museum and several other informed colonists that I was reasonably prepared to tackle this narrative account of the Colony through my wide acquaintance among leading artists and particularly because of the more than a score of taped interviews I had conducted with Provincetown painters of several generations, most for the Archives of American Art.

In 1975 when the initial planning for the Provincetown exhibition began, Ronald A. Kuchta and I were both aware of how little had been written on the colony from an art historical point of view. Articles on particular American colonies were apt to concentrate on personalities, bohemian frolics, picturesque scenery. Discussions of cheap living in the old days were part of the nostalgia, and the artist was seen as a more colorful vacationist with a penchant for shop talk with his cronies. Ross Moffett's valuable little book on the history of the Provincetown Art Association was an indispensable source but dealt only with artists in the organization, and its chronicle ended in 1947. Initially the exhibition planned for the Everson was to include about fifty painters who had worked in Provincetown from 1900 to about the later 1950's. The pressures to include more artists and to extend the period covered came only partially from the outside; there was the need to maintain balance and to be fair.

My interest in art colonies as a phenomenon had been aroused as early as the 1940's when I was lecturing on Gauguin. John Rewald's account of the colony at Pont Aven in Brittany offered tantalizing suggestions of artists affected in their work and in their lives by a kind of nature scenario, in that instance medieval and mystical. I was fascinated by the evidence that the artist's view and image of nature is highly subjective and also transformed by his cultural aspirations. Out of this came works in an original style by Gauguin and Bernard. At the same time, in the south of France, the countryside around Arles was being perceived and painted by Van Gogh as Japan — not a suggestion of Asia but the Japanese land itself — and this subjective conception was impelling him to purify his own highly individual style. In Barbizon decades before, the scenarios had been different but also very fruitful for painting.

In the early 1960's when, on an assignment from the Archives of American Art, I began making tapes of interviews with artists in Woodstock and in Provincetown, I seemed to have the field to myself. No one had made a comparative study of the American colonies or related them to the colonies in Europe. In Woodstock I soon stumbled upon the European connection again. The several founders of the colony, led initially by Ralph Radcliffe Whitehead, an English philanthropist and pupil of John Ruskin, had been inspired by Ruskin's dream of establishing Utopian communes. The invitation to write on Provincetown was all the more irresistible because of my notes on these trans-Atlantic examples. Tucked away in the appendix of this volume (with additions from recent publications on Taos and Sante Fe, Gloucester and Easthampton) are brief resumes based on these early researches on European and American colonies. They proved only tangentially helpful in shaping an account of Provincetown.

I soon found out that what I knew about Provincetown from my tapes and even from my long established contacts with artists was only the tip of the iceberg. For the remaining time-submerged material I would need to dig into unfamiliar documents and rely on fallible memories other than my own. Ross Moffett with his talk of Indian artifacts and burial grounds and his interest in the geology of the Cape headed me in the right direction for pre-Colony history. After my interviews with Karl Knaths I had re-read Thoreau's book on the Cape with its fascinating but very unromantic description of the rough huts and fish-drying "flakes," of a Provincetown with only the most improvised walkways to serve as streets. From Moffett, Knaths and later Dickinson I caught a glimpse of an early Provincetown that offered not escape or glamour but independence, roots, a chance to build.

With the outbreak of World War I there was an abrupt shift from Thoreau and Spartan simplicity to a bizarre Provincetown that had overnight become a surrogate for the Left Bank of Paris. Was there another colony where the problems of the world were being thrashed out on beaches and in studios by people like Jack Reed, by socialist poets and genial anarchists as well as artists? Painters were caught up in the political reverberations of the war and, especially after the Armory Show, by the shock waves of aesthetic rebellions launched in Europe. International personalities marched on and off the scene, some caught up for a while by the idealism and spontaneity of the Provincetown Players. It seemed to me, as I pored over the vivid recollections of Mary Heaton Vorse and Mabel Dodge, that it was the intensity of the Players and their participating artist friends that most illuminated this period. The example of their close communal creativity offered a scenario greater than any they presented on the stage. It was like a partial fulfillment of Van Gogh's dream that artists, living together close to nature, would be able to create something through shared effort, greater than any of them could have achieved by himself alone.

Another side of this period was dramatized in the excesses of what Stuart Davis called (if memory serves me) the "go to hell-ers." With all the hard drinking of bootlegged liquor, and the tangle of torrid love affairs, it is surprising that nevertheless enough painting was done to fill the Town Hall exhibitions of the newly founded Art Association and even to spill over into smaller shows.

By now I was resigned to a decade-by-decade narrative since it seemed that Provincetown changed not only its cast of characters but also its mood, aesthetic outlook and even its appearance about every ten years. Faced with the proliferation of organized activities in the 1920's, with traditionalists and moderns, led by rival groups of expatriates, confronting each other, with the newly-housed Art Association splitting apart, I wondered what had become of the simple life, free of city tensions, dreamed by various colony founders. Yet even as the opposed factions moved to set up their separate juries and shows, they were all being affected by a new outlook and changing objectives. With ruler and compass and via mathematical formulae, one faction derived its aesthetic from the Golden Section and Dynamic Symmetry, while the other took its direction from Cubist authorities. Everyone was intent on producing the perfect picture. Just when they thought they had the hang of it, they were overtaken by the Depression and all objectives changed. The search was on for a type of realism that would encompass the realities of the American Scene. Provincetown, which had looked rather European to the Barbizon-inspired Impressionists around Hawthorne, and which had looked to Europe for ideas in the 1920's, appeared in the 1930's to have rejoined the American continent in appearance and state of mind.

The towering figure of this period was Edward Hopper, an artist with whom I had talked late in his career and not in the context of the Cape. He had lived on the periphery of an art colony (and before that Gloucester with trips to the New Mexico colonies), while in his life and work flouting every preconception of the colonist as a romantic escapist, high-living and gregarious. In his painting, he favored seedy decay over scenic charm, he avoided meetings and was rarely seen at Provincetown parties. In the household maintained by his vivacious but abstemious wife in their almost inaccessible hilltop house, the Baba Rhum cakes served neighbors at occasional teas never contained a drop of rum.

Each time a new aesthetic concept took over, there was a displacement of established styles and reputations — a gain and a loss. The most drastic displacement of all was probably the one that began during World War II, gained momentum in the years following the war's end, and swept into a tidal wave in the 1950's. Where before I had been struggling to piece together from various sources the shape of the woods — the colony as a whole — now I could see only the trees, the individual Abstract Expressionists I had known from first hand experience. It turned out that my memory was just as treacherous as any. In Provincetown I had continued an acquaintance with "Miz" and Hans Hofmann begun in the early 1950's when I was writing an article for *Art News* on the Hofmann School in New York. In talks with Hofmann I was often aware of a striking difference from the Abstract Expressionists in his way of thinking about nature as a source for art. Since Hofmann had told me once in a serious mood, that his best students were those who turned against him, it was interesting to learn in recent talks with some of these one-time rebels, that they increasingly recognized the significance of his teaching.

Through a rich cache of materials lent by Esther Gottlieb (including letters from Welden Kees), I was able to reconstruct the lively and intense debates of Forum '49, and in a taped interview, Judith Rothschild and Fritz Bultman recalled the warmth, the intense exchanges and also the shared aspirations of that time. This camaraderie among the Abstract Expressionists was not to survive the spectacular success (accompanied by art world manipulations) of the later 1950's.

The glow of hopeful community enterprise passed in the latter 1950's to the struggling young artists — restless under the hegemony of abstraction, who gathered to show their paintings, poems, constructions, and as yet unnamed "happenings" in the miniscule Sun Gallery. Ranging from the roughest of improvised figures to the haunting tableaux of heroes' and hexes painted by Jan Müller, the Sun's art fare was a sign of another stylistic displacement in the making. This time the artists being nudged off the stage were the Abstract Expressionists and even Hofmann. But the Sun was too small to weigh immediately in the power structure of the Colony. The impact of this challenge would not be felt until the 1960's and then in New York.

The effort to check and verify an avalanche of material on recent decades has to be halted by our deadline, and as this goes to press I am haunted by omissions and loose ends. Since this project was undertaken, several now and well-prepared and very interesting publications on art colonies have been published and it can be expected that other scholars will turn to this field. With this untidy first over-all chronicle on Provincetown on hand, it can be hoped that they will be able to correct the mistakes and fill in the gaps.

Origins — Provincetown and the Cape End

The glaciers that thrust the sands beneath Provincetown more than sixty miles out into the Atlantic, insured its brilliant sunlight — unmatched this side of Greece. The Cape tip, whipped into its sickle shape by turbulent winds and seas, was to

Aerial view of Provincetown — Courtesy of the Provincetown Advocate.

be volatile in its history too, different in its inhabitants from both the mainland and the rest of the Cape.

The legend that the Viking Thorvald had landed there around 1000 A.D. was given some substance when, in the course of excavations in the mid-19th century, a wall of large stones of a type unknown on the Cape, but possibly like those used for ballast on Viking ships was found under Provincetown's Chip Hill. By the end of the fifteenth century reports of the astonishingly abundant fish of Georges Banks had reached Europe; vessels from England, Portugal, Norway and France were anchored in Provincetown's Bay. In 1602 one Bartholomew Gosnold, an English navigator, gave the peninsula the name "Cape Cod" as a tribute to schools of fish so thick that mariners (Sebastian Cabot in the late 1400's) had often reported their vessels unable to make headway.

About 1000 B.C. Cape Cod was inhabited by tribes of hunters of unknown origin whose quartz arrowheads have been found. Around 1 A.D. they were succeeded by tribes probably of the Algonquin linguistic stock, who ate oysters and quahaugs, had some knowledge of horticulture, and shaped storage vessels of clay.

The Indian inhabitants of the Cape End at the time of the Pilgrim landing, members of the powerful Wampanoag Federation, were headed by the great chief, Massasoit, in command of an army of more than six thousand warriers from tribes based on the Cape, Rhode Island, Plymouth and other parts of the mainland — a total population estimated at about 35,000. It was an army that he needed since he was situated between the powerful Narragansetts on one side and the almost equally strong Massachusetts on the other. Although the Indians soon became friendly and were to adopt the Pilgrims' clothing, tools, weapons and utensils, a band unsuccessfully attacked an exploring party sent out by the Pilgrims. This initial hostility can be attributed to the fact that the Indians had been cheated, tricked, and also captured and sold as slaves in Europe by European traders who preyed on them for decades before the Mayflower arrived. When this first party of Pilgrim explorers stumbled on one of the many Indian burial grounds scattered over the Cape (some still survive and have not been excavated), they plundered it for the seed-corn the Indians customarily buried for use in the life to come. The burial site was Corn Hill, now much favored by artists for its view.

Provincetown continues to smart from the failure of most historical accounts to note that the Pilgrims landed on its shore and conducted substantial explorations five weeks before they landed in Plymouth. In 1907, to set the record straight and commemorate the event, the town, liberally assisted by State and Federal funds, began to erect, on the hill behind Town Hall, the Pilgrim Monument towering 252 feet and, for no logical reason, designed as a near duplicate of a tower in Sienna, Italy.

The Pilgrims sailed the Mayflower into Provincetown Harbor on November 11, 1620 (Old Style reckoning). As they dropped anchor, William Bradford was concerned about some reports of "discontented and mutinous speeches;" he summoned all aboard to sign the Mayflower Compact in order to "covenant and combine ourselves together into a civil body politick, for our better ordering and preservation ... " No one since has been more successful in heading off the disruptions of the unruly in Provincetown.

In the following centuries, the Cape End was the refuge and sometimes home of restless and rootless men of the sea. The farmers who settled the rest of the Cape including the more staid people of Truro, said they were godless and ordered that churches be built. In the past as in the present, the economy of Provincetown has rested on the fishing fleet, trawlers and seine-fishing, and the related trades. The products of the whaling industry made the town prosperous in the 19th century. In the early decades the great whalers were owned and manned by seamen of Yankee stock who also dominated in the general

Schooners in the Harbor, with Methodist Church — Provincetown, Massachusetts.
Photograph courtesy of Cyril Patrick

population of the town. From ports in the Azores the whaling ships usually picked up a large part of their crews, Portuguese seamen — often gotten aboard for years-long voyages by tricks and even by outright "shanghaing." They had no compunction about jumping ship once they were in port. Those who came to Provincetown in this way discovered a place to their liking; as fishermen they could make a far better living than in the home country. They settled down and had large families; by 1875 they outnumbered the Yankee natives. The narrow streets of the town acquired a new picturesqueness and flavor from the speech, food, costumes and folkways of a dark-eyed, olive-skinned Mediterranean people. Their presence in the town was to be as much an attraction to artists as the landscape, and on their part the Portuguese were more inclined to accept the unconventional ways of artists than the staid New Englanders.

The railroad reached Provincetown in 1873, a quarter of a century after Henry David Thoreau had predicted that easy access by rail would turn the towns of the Cape into summer resorts. Along with the vacationers, several artists began summering in Provincetown, among them William F. Halsall (1841–1919), a dignified old time marine artist who painted (in the shirt factory building on Court Street) a 30-foot canvas of the battleship Oregon making its spectacular voyage around the Horn in 1898. William Paxton (1869–1941), a "name" artist from Boston drove down in one of the earliest automobiles to be seen on the Cape End. In 1900 the American Impressionist, Childe Hassam, painted *Provincetown Grocery Store.* The building has been identified as one erected in 1799. Prior to becoming a grocery it had been a cobbler's shop with a back room where the gentry gathered to settle the affairs of the town over a bottle and a pipe. Messages for the Town Crier were written on a small slate which hung beside the door to be "cried" the length of the town "up-along" and "down-along."

In 1901 there were eight hotels and many more boarding houses. One of the most popular was the Figurehead House — the upper half of the handsomely carved maiden still leans with calm brow over the traffic of Commercial Street. It typified the genteel boarding houses ready to accommodate the young ladies who began arriving by the dozens to study with Charles W. Hawthorne. The rent was cheap — meals for about twenty cents — and there was an understanding that no one would make a fuss about the lack of plumbing. Male students were handy at converting old fish sheds into studio-quarters. Or, for fifty dollars a year, they could rent a studio in the attached second story line built above Days Lumber Yard. Artists made it a habit to hang around at dockside when the fleet was returning to unload; they could walk off with the makings of a dinner from fish amiably tossed by the crew, ostensibly to be painted as still-life subjects.

But even the advantage of cheap living, unsurpassed light, appealing landscape and all the colorful residues of its picaresque history would not necessarily have produced the enduring nucleus of a colony without the presence of those who called on young painters and sculptors to seek the life of the true artist. From the turn of the century there was never a decade when there was not a teacher of extraordinary gifts in Provincetown to extoll the life in art as superior, a calling for the chosen.

Hawthorne and the Cape Cod School 1899–1930

The founding of the Cape Cod School in Provincetown came about in part because of a falling out between two teachers whose esthetic ideas were to be germinal to the colony; one, *William Merritt Chase* (1849–1916), was probably the most highly regarded and sought after master at the National Academy and also at the Art Students League, the other, *Charles Webster Hawthorne* (1872–1930), was already an accomplished young painter and valued teaching assistant for the Chase classes.

Painting on the beach. — Circa 1910 — Photograph courtesy of Cyril Patrick

20

At the turn of the century a diluted form of impressionism was coming into vogue and the master who exploited it most skillfully—adding the embellishment of a Sargentesque brush (he called it "le morceau bien fait")—was the popular and successful William Merritt Chase. He charmed everyone with his debonair manner, fashionable dress and deft demonstrations. Under the spell of Chase, young Hawthorne turned away from the more traditional training he had received at the Art Students League under Dumond, Brush and Mowbray, and embraced the new mode.

Chase recognized Hawthorne's exceptional talents as a teacher as well as a painter. When Chase returned in the summer of 1897 to the summer art school he had opened the previous year at Shinnecock Hills (Southhampton), he took Hawthorne along as an assistant, and found him a place to stay in a shack used to store fishermen's gear. As the son of a sea captain (he had grown up in the seaport town of Richmond, Maine), Hawthorne felt at home in the marine surroundings; moreover, he had an opportunity in his closer relationship with Chase to observe at first hand every aspect of the functioning of a summer art school.

A close but troubled friendship grew up between the two men. Hawthorne had every reason to expect that he would be asked to take over the school in the event that Chase, always in demand as the Art Student League's most prestigious teacher and at the very hub of art world activities, should have to give up his summer classes.

In the summer of 1898 Hawthorne was leaving for Holland on a study trip, when he heard the shocking news that Chase had closed his school in Southampton; the property had been sold to Douglas John Connah. In spite of this crushing disappointment he did not abandon his idea of a summer art school in a seaside environment. The following year he came to Provincetown, the fishing village he remembered vividly from a brief, earlier visit, and founded the Cape Cod School of Art.

Although several artists from Boston had already discovered Provincetown and in the 1890's were summering there, it was not their presence that attracted Hawthorne to the place—actually his attention had been called to the town by a physician friend. As an unspoiled fishing village, only marginally a tourist haven and still inexpensive for its accommodations, it was an ideal setting for a school that was to attract young people from all over the country. The fact that there was much in the look and flavor of Provincetown that recalled the old fishing villages of Europe added to its appeal for young artists who at that time could only imagine the true artist's life as beginning across the Atlantic. Hawthorne was also oriented to Europe; in Provincetown's population of Portuguese with a vivid history as seafarers he was to find a subject matter that would hold his interest over a lifetime.

He married Ethel Marion Campbell whom he had met when she was the secretary at the Chase school. A large frame house built early in the century atop Miller Hill, with a sweeping view over rooftops to the Bay, became the Hawthorne's home as well as accommodations for the school. In the early years classes met in the two largest rooms; as the school expanded, a barn-like structure was added at the north end.

On sunny days the class model would be posed (clothed) on one of the open wharves then scattered all along the harbor front. According to Hawthorne's directives she would be seated in the full glare of the sun with her face shaded either by a hat or parasol, producing on the canvases of the students a typical image that came to be called "the Mudhead." Hawthorne's strategy was to force students to grasp the form through the contrast of illuminated and shadowed parts. Unable to see facial features and other details which would have preoccupied them ordinarily, they escaped the distractions that would have kept them from grasping the total image in its broadest terms. One of his more famous

Charles Hawthorne teaching painting on the wharf

students, Edwin Dickinson, has explained Hawthorne's emphasis on painting in brilliant sunlight as a means of training students to distinguish closely related tones such as a lemon yellow and an ochre yellow which are most easily seen at the top of the palette. What Hawthorne wanted them to see was not the beauty of a face or form but, in his words: "the beauty of one spot of color coming against another." In this constantly reiterated advice Hawthorne was not speaking of the kinds of daubs and color touches that would cover the surface of a typical French impressionist painting, of a Monet or Renoir, but of the larger contrasts in color tones.

The Impressionism that Chase had adopted and passed on to Hawthorne was not the mature style inspired by the full spectrum of hues seen in the work of Claude Monet and other French Impressionists in the late 1870's and 1880's. The Chase style stemmed from a pictorial formula that first developed in France in the 1860's and was transmitted to Germany where it became the basis for a dark (tonal) impressionism, taught first in Dusseldorf, then in Munich. The Bavarian painter, Wilhelm Leibl, who had been influenced by Gustav Courbet was a model for the style that brought success to Frank Duveneck's own school of Munich. Chase was one of the "Duveneck boys," who succeeded in making this form of impressionism acceptable by about 1914 to the National Academy.

Another Hawthorne student, Ross Moffett remembered that in the teens the talk of students in Hawthorne's class was not about the French moderns (although they had attracted wide attention in the Armory Show) but about the Spaniards, Zuloaga and Sorolla, whose dramatic, colorful styles were then popular among Americans.

Nevertheless Hawthorne was an innovator in his classroom techniques. In requiring students to work not with brushes but with blunt-ended putty knives, he was moving against the kind of showy technique for its own sake that Chase had encouraged. In a series of very interesting letters written to his wife-to-be from Holland in 1898, Hawthorne described his despair as he tried repeatedly to emulate the brush strokes of his idol, Franze Hals. Eventually he realized that his attention to the brush was in fact the obstacle that prevented his dealing with the large essential forms. In an effort to forestall this kind of false virtuosity he sometimes told students they could apply paint even with their fingers, "Go out like a savage, as if paint had just been invented."

His weekly demonstration class was held out of doors in good weather and often as many as one hundred gathered on the wharf or beach to watch what was sure to be superb performance. The model was posed by his assistant, and on Hawthorne's huge palette mounds of color laid out in precise sequence. His pipe was also in readiness for the master. Dressed impeccably in white flannels the teacher appeared, graciously accepted the palette and the long brushes that, in his case, were allowed. In a very short time and in a way that seemed almost magical, the forms materialized on the canvas, color spot by color spot. It has been said by Hawthorne's son, Jo (now the conductor of the Duluth Symphony), that it was possible, in looking at these studies years later, to determine from the figure the exact hour and weather of the day and even the direction of the wind.

According to all reports students appeared at the weekly Saturday morning criticisms weak-kneed and prepared for the worst in an unsparing canvas by canvas review that lasted several hours. In examining these student efforts — each consisting of a few masses of color applied thickly with the palette knife — Hawthorne paid no attention to drawings or to composition in the sense of a deliberate structuring of elements. There was stern reproach for the pupil bent on pretty effects, praise for the one that had extracted "delicious" juxtapositions of color from a commonplace, or better yet, from an ugly subject (an old tin can on the beach). Ridicule and some lampooning titles were in store for the beginner who turned up with a seascape.

Above all the praiseworthy painting must register an excitement that carried the novice beyond the usual reasonable turn of mind. "Painters don't reason, they do," said Hawthorne. "The moment they reason they are lost — subconscious thought counts... Suppose music were all a thin piping without anything hoary or grisly that reaches down to the emotions?"

Hawthorne was expressing attitudes that, three decades later, were to be central to the credo of the Abstract-Expressionists; no wonder that Hofmann, who never knew Hawthorne, detected in his words and work "a cataclysmic temperament." In both of Hawthorne's roles there was the implication of strong forces held in tension.

In somewhat the same way as Hans Hofmann, who was to follow him, Hawthorne held before the student the idea that a life in art was a means of self-transformation, the serious artist joined a select, timeless company of inspired beings with a shared version of "the beauty and the glory of human existence." He told the class: "The only way that he (the painter) can appeal to humanity is in the guise of the high priest."

Hawthorne was in every way equipped to play this role. A man of imposing stature, he projected majesterial authority and a magnetic presence — the image of a master. Although he had known hard work making his way as an art student on his own financially in New York (he worked on the docks and in a stained glass factory) in Provincetown his life style, with the family always dressing for dinner in elaborately oak-paneled rooms, was aristocratic.

At the turn of the century (before he fell under Italian Renaissance influence) Hawthorne was painting the Portuguese with a vigorous Halsian realism barely matched at the time by Robert Henri and *The Eight.* In his large *Cleaning Fish* so exact are the purplish flesh tones of the upward-glancing Portuguese named Silva in the foreground, that it was possible for scientists to deduce that the man was suffering from a skin disease common to those whose hands are daily plunged into fish innards.

On an extended trip to Italy in 1906, he was deeply affected by Titian, Perugino and other Renaissance masters. Hawthorne's subjects became more idealized, his earlier sharp lights and shadows were replaced by evenly graduated tones, softly defining simplified contours and broad, flattened planes. Surfaces were elaborately built up and often scumbled in a process of using dry pigment mixed with a substance Hawthorne believed had been Tintoretto's medium but which time has proved unstable. (It was manufactured by Eimer and Amend, and called "Hawthorne's medium.")

As his reputation as a society portraitist soared, so did his fees. He hated most of these commissions, but accepted a good many at $4,000 each. In 1911 Hawthorne received an unprecedented honor from the National Academy when his *The Trousseau* (now in the Metropolitan) was awarded the Thomas B. Clark prize on the first ballot. In 1924 his psychologically compelling *The Captain's Wife* was awarded the Carnegie Prize "for most meritorious painting."

Continued stubbornly through his later career in the face of much criticism was "the Hawthorne stare." The eyes of his frontally-positioned subjects were painted looking toward the viewer, yet often seemed turned inward in reverie. In a memorable painting like his *The Family* the Portuguese subjects looking away from their world into ours, assume an aspect of timelessness. "The stare" in his painting of young girls accentuates a duality: they seem delicately sensual yet so withdrawn as to suggest a Puritan repressiveness. In the portrait of his friend, the artist and plainsman John Noble (1930), the stare is a foil to the subject's genial slouch and roguish expression.

Hawthorne, who had turned out so many fine landscapists from his classes, had seldom painted landscape himself. He proved that he had a remarkable eye for what John Marin called "the big forms" in landscape as well as a command of

Sargentesque technique in the last year of his life. On a trip to the Azores and to France and Spain, he took along his watercolors. While his family visited a church he would sweep running washes across the paper with a headlong rush, fusing the essentials of sky and earth in a total image at once airy, vast and mysterious.

In addition to Edwin Dickinson and Ross Moffett, a number of other artists who studied with Hawthorne sunk roots into the Cape End and Provincetown. Active in the Art Association, often continuing to teach and exhibit, they have provided a continuity. Among those who have lived in the area year-round: Henry Hensche, Reeves Euler, Bruce McKain, Philip Malicoat, George Yater, Courtney Allen, and Joe Kaplan.

Those who have settled into summer homes where they usually spend almost six months of the year include: Jerry Farnsworth, Helen Sawyer, Jack Tworkov who studied with Hawthorne in New York, and Marjorie Windust. Based in Paris for many years, Janice Biala usually returns to Provincetown for a few weeks each summer.

Early Schools: E. Ambrose Webster

Ambrose Webster (1869–1935), a descendant of Daniel Webster, has been described by Ross Moffett as the indisputable "pioneer of modernism" of the Cape. Indeed, Webster was an ardent and respected spokesman for avant-garde theories during his lifetime in Provincetown. He founded his Summer School of Painting in 1900 after two years of study in Paris, where he was deeply affected by the Impressionist paintings he discovered on his own (not at the Academie Julian where his teachers were Benjamin Constant and Jean Paul Laurens). In the first decade there seem to have been few students on the Cape fired with a desire to master the fully coloristic Impressionism that interested Webster. The purple shadows laced through his paintings of trees were even more of a scandal than the fact that he was to be an exhibitor at the notorious Armory Show that introduced modernism to this country.

A small, shy man, he is vividly remembered by Helen Sawyer: "Webster was like a character out of a story book," she writes, "with his bicycle bell and lisping voice. He was honest and very appealing." One of the founding members of the Art Association, he was one of its first vice presidents and served as director in 1917, 1918 and 1919.

In the summers he was occupied earnestly explaining his modern art theories at his school and in lectures, but in winters he took off from his Bradford Street home for long painting sojourns abroad, usually in tropical countries. There the blaze of sunlight on tropical foliage brought delight in patterns and heightened contrasts. After another year's study in Paris in the early 1920's, he focused more on architectural forms in landscape. When he died in Provincetown in 1935 he left behind a body of his travel paintings that are just now being rediscovered.

Art Schools

By the summer of 1916, there were five summer art schools in Provincetown. In addition to the schools of Hawthorne and Webster, one that was to flourish for decades was the West End School run by landscapist *George Elmer Browne* (1871–1946) at a structure on a high hill. Browne's open, genial manner and his emphasis on lively composition made him a popular teacher. In the winter he often conducted students to Europe for extended study and painting sojourns. Another school called A Modern School of Art, lasted only two seasons in spite of its outstanding faculty: Bror J. O. Norfeldt, William Zorach and his wife,

Outdoor painting class from the figure — Circa 1910 — Photograph courtesy of
Cyril Patrick

Marguerite Zorach, Frederick Burt (all four active Provincetown Players), and also M. Musselman Carr. For two seasons a class in monochrome and color etching run by George Sensany, reflected the interest in print making that never quite left Provincetown.

The activities of the Provincetown Print Makers (launched in 1915) were stimulated by an innovation introduced by Bror J. O. Norfeldt (1878–1955): he demonstrated that by cutting a fine line around shapes, a number of different colors could be printed from the same woodblock. This stylization was readily acceptable to most of the group since most of its members were oriented to abstraction and already using flattened areas in their work. Printing with watercolor they obtained a lyric, airy effect with generally light, cool hues. Among those showing before 1920 either in the Art Association or in the gallery they maintained for a time in a building located where the Post Office now stands were: the pioneering geometric abstractionist, Blanche Lazzell and Karl Knaths, Agnes Weinrich, Maude Squire, Ellen Ravenscroft, Ada Gilmore Chaffee, Ethel Mars, Mildred MacMillan, Tod Lindenmuth, Juliette S. Nichols and Maud Ainslie. This print enterprise flourished into the twenties and after decades when it disappeared from the local scene it was revived by Ferol Warthen, Angele Myrer, and Hope Voorhees Pfeiffer.

World War I: Expatriates Return

In the winter of 1914, Hawthorne was enjoying a working sojourn in Paris. He had taken a studio on the Boulevard St. Jacques, and was part of a circle of distinguished American expatriates. After war broke out, several of them recalled Hawthorne's warm endorsement of Provincetown and its advantages for the painter. One by one they closed their ateliers and made their way to the Cape End to be welcomed as befitted artists who had made enviable reputations abroad, exhibited and won honors in the Paris salons, and had either earned, or were in line for, election to the American Academy of Design.

The willingness of the new arrivals to serve as officers of the newly formed Provincetown Art Association won enthusiastic approval from a large part of the colony, but some of the young rebels who had been stirred by the revelations of the 1913 Armory Show, saw the academicians as pillars of the status quo.

The expatriates themselves, although they had perhaps not moved in circles where the name of Cezanne was revered, did not regard themselves as "old hat." When they were coming of age as artists, academic training in Europe was the only possible entry into the National Academy, and the National Academy was the only place to exhibit where the work would be taken seriously by critics and connoisseurs. Once in Europe, basking in the regard of art celebrities, the path of least resistance was to become more attuned to the prevalent classicism with its goddesses, arcadias and madonnas than to struggle to maintain an American identity. Most of the Americans in Paris had made gingerly advances toward newer currents of tradition; they studied the broad brushwork of Velasquez and the simplified tonalities of the early Manet; some absorbed aspects of Impressionists. The palettes of Richard Miller, John Noble and George Elmer Browne had been freshened by addition of Impressionism's brighter, cooler tones; Max Bohm seldom departed from the "dark impressionism" associated with Frank Duveneck in Munich.

Max Bohm (1868–1923) was an impressive man, dashing and handsome as a young man in Paris, rugged and self-assured in middle age when he came to Provincetown in 1917 (he was 49 and the father of two daughters who were to grow up there). Born in 1868, Bohm was the son of a well to do family recently transplanted from Germany to Cleveland. At 19 he was sent off to Europe for art

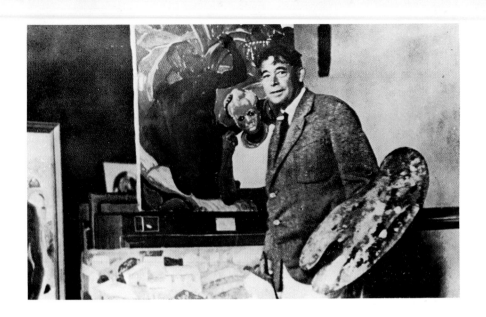

E. Ambrose Webster in his studio

study with Jean Paul Laurens, in the charge of a favorite aunt. When he was 25, his paintings were being shown regularly at the Paris salons. He had a fashionable portrait clientele, and patrons who bought his mythological or dramatic subjects and his paintings of madonna-like mothers and children.

In Provincetown he built a substantial house at the top of a steep hill, in the extreme East End, and converted an old barn into a studio. He was a force in the town, a respected figure in the Art Association until his sudden, untimely death in 1923. His wife and two daughters continued to live in Provincetown.

Bohm made honest, incisive drawings of the intimate world of his home, penetrating, golden-toned portraits of himself and his children, airy symbolic paintings of muses and even of Mary Baker Eddy. The subjects that elicited his boldest, most inspired brush, were fashionable women in voluminous hats, wind-blown and dramatically lighted as they strolled out-of-doors.

When *John Noble* (1874–1934) arrived in 1919, the focus of attention was on his five-gallon Stetson hat, on his legend as a son of the prairie wilderness, and on his stories about having driven cattle on the old Chisholm Trail. There was so much response to his jovial personality and gossip over his hard-drinking nights, that very few noticed his genuine response to American art. He was perhaps the only one among the returning expatriates to be interested in what had been going on among native painters in his absence. Ross Moffett reports that when Noble was shown landscapes by some Americans (it would be interesting to know whose) he exclaimed, "Why there's nothing like this in Europe — America will save the world for art." This was from a man who had seen a great deal of European art during his twenty-five years of living abroad, and had produced a respectable amount of work himself. He knew the hothouse academic product as it was turned out in the capitals of Europe, and it was clear to him that something else was needed.

Noble's tenure (early 1920's) as first director of the Art Association, after it moved into its permanent quarters in the new building, is recalled with affection by artists of all stylistic stripes; he got along well with everyone. Young Jack Tworkov, counted among the young rebels in his search for a new direction, liked him at first meeting at the Beachcombers, where Noble often drank with Eugene O'Neill, John Dos Passos, and was occasionally gently subdued by Hawthorne.

Between his bouts of flamboyant socializing, Noble did work in his studio on paintings that express a very different side of himself, a side as gentle as his public image was picaresque. In his landscapes, sea and shore are seen under a veiled sun or misty moon and invested with mystical feeling. Even when he tackled the obviously dramatic subject of *The Wreck* (reproduced on the cover of *Art News,* February 1935) he avoided histrionics, focusing on the white horse — a favorite motif — that would pull the hull ashore. Noble's romanticism was agreeably understated. His seas do not roar and plunge, but receive the light in a scalloped flow of mellow color.

Perhaps after his massive dose of European academicism, Noble's experience with freshly-seen native paintings was a kind of aesthetic homecoming, a happy signal for the shedding of a suffocating artificiality.

Hawthorne painted a vital, psychologically penetrating portrait of his friend, John Noble; the last portrait completed before Hawthorne's death in 1930, possibly his strongest. Four years later, Noble was dead of alcoholism in a New York hospital. Hawthorne's famous portrait device of "the stare," was particularly effective here, capturing something in the almost defiant expression of the eyes that seems to contradict the rueful and roguish smile.

George Elmer Browne (1871–1946) was an outstandingly successful landscape painter and vintage bohemian character in Provincetown from the teens until he died there in 1946. His watercolors were as skillful and popular as his oils; in either medium the challenge for Browne was to capture the drama of a place. He was not content as were most of his academic friends, to pose a model and fill in a landscape background from imagination. His style required the handling of people and place as a unit, equally saturated with light, moving to the identical rhythm; crowds at the Corrida under a blazing sun, peasants exploring the curiosities of circus grounds, or Arabs gathered in a market place of Tangier. This meant on-the-spot sketching (with painting done in the studio) on the Cape or in Brittany, Spain, Corsica, Venice, the Basque country and the Gaspé.

After growing up in Salem, Massachusetts (he was born in Baltimore) and early study at the Boston Museum Art School, he took off for Paris and enrolled at the Academy Julian where his masters were Jules Lefebre and Tony Robert-Fleury. A friend's early portrait shows him bearded, wearing his beret at a jaunty angle; the international cafe diversions of the Left Bank were "made to order" to gratify a nature as extroverted and fond of socializing as his. His foreign honors came early and late; in 1904 the French government bought *Bait Sellers of Cape Cod;* and he was made a Chevalier of the French Legion of Honor in 1926, at a time when he was conducting art classes in Paris.

By the early 1920's, the directness and dramatic emphasis of Browne's style was acceptable to the National Academy (which made him a member in 1923, a full academician in 1928), but in 1917 when he was given a one man show at Knoedler, a critic chided him for his aggressive attack: "All these large canvases appear positively to elbow each other in their insistent claim on the spectator's attention."

In spite of his globe trotting, he usually managed to get back to spend the summer in the ample, specially-designed studio he had built on a hilltop in the West End (it later became the home of another equally colorful character, the sculptor, Chaim Gross). There in the early years he conducted his West End School, emphasizing composition to his students at a time when this was unusual. Wearing his natty white cotton hat he was a perennial party-goer, and most happily in his element at the annual Beachcomber's clambake.

Browne served on the committee that wrote the constitution of the Art Association in 1921, and was also an Honorary Vice-President that year. He proposed the creation of a Hawthorne Memorial Gallery in 1930. A year before he died in 1946, he was a member of a panel leading a discussion on *"What has Art to do with Life?"*

Of the Americans established abroad who arrived in the teens, *Richard E. Miller* (1875–1943), a native of St. Louis, was the most coloristically impressionist in style, yet the most bitterly anti-modern in attitude. Attractive models were always in demand at his spacious East End studio which was set back from Bradford Street above a verdant hollow. This heavily-timbered, two-story building was one of those floated across from Long Point on scows (later it became the home of painter Irving Marantz). His success in Paris was apparently based on paintings of models posed as fashionable ladies in the boudoir, or other bourgeois surroundings that would allow for the play of sunlight on comely flesh, on ribbons and ornaments. Yet when Miller could set aside the contrived artificiality of this kind of marketable fare, he was capable of considerable depth and sensitivity. This is seen in his sympathetically affectionate portrait of young Edwin (Eddie) Reeves Euler, with the stuffed owl (which Eddie still owns) crowning the subtle composition. During the depression years, Miller held an important post dispensing jobs and commissions for the WPA as area director.

One of the earliest artists to summer in Provincetown, and a distinguished member of the colony for decades, was *William Paxton* (1869–1941) who became a full academician early in his career. Like his friend, George Elmer Browne, he had grown up in Massachusetts, and studied and exhibited in Paris (his master was Gerome, the neo-classical salon favorite). But, where Browne had developed a bravura manner, Paxton perfected two styles, one of smooth, jewel-like surfaces, the other a more fluid technique with free, animated brush strokes. Some of his best-known paintings aspire to the manner of Vermeer. His preferred subjects were patrician ladies quietly disposed in elegant, contemporary surroundings; his compositions were serenely ordered in a structural framework. Apparently the old and new rich families of Beacon Hill found in them some ideal they claimed as their own; they snapped up his paintings at very high prices. Paxton was the only artist in pre-war Provincetown to own an automobile.

Another type of expatriate returned to native shores not crowned with laurels from academies abroad but inspired by the pioneering innovations of Cezanne and the Cubists or possibly the Fauves. Among them was *Agnes Weinrich,* sister of the musician, Helen Weinrich (Mrs. Karl Knaths). Born in Burlington, Iowa, she studied in art schools in Paris and Berlin before 1914 and returned to the United States at the outbreak of the First World War. After a period of study at the Chicago Art Institute, she came to Provincetown and enrolled in the classes of Hawthorne. She was deeply influenced by the Armory Show and subsequently attracted by the abstract forms being developed by artists in the group championed by Alfred Stieglitz. Living in Provincetown year round for most of her mature life, she was active in the Art Association. She had one man shows of her vigorously abstract paintings in Boston, Washington and Chicago before her death in 1946.

Blanche Lazzell (18 ?–1956), one of the most remarkable figures in the annals of Provincetown, is known to have studied in Paris with Fernand Leger, Andre Lhote and Albert Gleizes. Born near Maidsville, West Virginia, she became a Provincetown resident in 1915. Outwardly appearing a lady unlikely to be associated with radical aesthetic causes or bohemian ways, she quietly developed her authoritative, non-objective paintings without any evidence of groping through semi-abstraction or intermediate styles. Like the works of the early Cubists, her canvases are subdued in color with browns, tans, blacks predominant. Her boldly interlocking shapes have the clean edges of ruler and compass composition. Surviving such early colleagues as Weinrich and Ambrose Webster, she was still vigorously at work in 1949 when her abstractions were singled out for critical praise in the initial exhibition of Forum '49. In the following decade she was deeply interested in the theories of Hans Hofmann.

Important among the avant-garde expatriates was *Oliver Chaffee* (1881–1944). Ross Moffett wrote: "There should be somewhere ... a body of Chaffee oil and watercolor landscapes that would represent one of the highest achievements realized by a Provincetown painter ... He was a modern before modernism was popular." Oliver Chaffee had already studied with Robert Henri and earlier with Frank Duveneck when he came to Provincetown in 1910 perhaps initially for study with Hawthorne. But he soon formed ties with Ambrose Webster who would have sympathized with Chaffee's growing interest in the French Fauves. By 1913 they were friends and equals, showing together by invitation at the famous Armory Show. Chaffee bought a house and lived in Provincetown year round except for trips abroad. If he was tempted into some eclecticism by repeated stays in Paris, his work was generally centered in the concepts of Matisse. The *New York Sun*'s prestigious critic, Henry McBride, spoke of Chaffee's "smashing his points home," and the *Times* called Chaffee an American Fauve. Moderns in the colony regarded Chaffee as a mentor. When he died in Provincetown in 1944, he was honored by a memorial exhibition of his work in the Hawthorne Gallery.

Abraham Walkowitz (1880–1965), whose rhythmically alive delineations of the figure were shown at Stieglitz's "291," had been inspired by the drawings of Matisse and Rodin. He is thought to have been in Provincetown a number of times probably during the late teens and early 1920's when he was turning out some of his most admired drawings. His nude girls or lightly draped figures, executed in line and airy pastels, moved in and out of grasses and waves with

Beachcomber and Art Association group, Provincetown Tercentenary parade,
1920. Left to right: Melzar Chaffee, in cloth cap, Gerrit Beneker, I. H. Caliga in
straw hat, W. H. W. Bicknell, William L'Engle in sweater, Ben Katz in cap, Harry
Campbell with bow tie, Thomas Hanford, Frederick Marvin with dark mustache,
George Elmer Brown, Frank Desch, E. Ambrose Webster behind flag, Max Bohm
in straw hat, Joseph Birren, S. Chatwood Burton, John Noble.

the same fluid intensity that marks his famous drawings of the "divine" Isadora Duncan. Walkowitz is listed among exhibitors in the separate modern shows of the Art Association during the 1927–1936 split.

First World War: Theater and Bohemia

The almost overnight change that transformed Provincetown in 1914 from a quiet fishing village into an extension of Greenwich Village and a surrogate for the Left Bank of Paris, has been variously reported; the word "invasion" appears in most accounts. Nothing less is adequate to describe the sudden influx of poets, novelists, journalists, celebrated bohemians, socialites and radicals of all stripes as well as critics and dilettantes. There was also a new, more citified type of painter. Many found cheap lodgings with fishermen's families; some wound up in dune shacks and a few renovated fish shacks on old wharves.

Hutchins Hapgood wrote (in his *A Victorian in the Modern World*) that even before the actual outbreak of war, "That summer marked a strange union of unlike elements, and yet a real union." He described the day that war was declared when people gathered in the local stationery store where papers were sold (Patrick's?): "The War went to our heads the whiskey helping merely to set free the emotional results from the War ... [the artists] felt the war as social upheaval rather than war ... it was personal and impersonal, a turmoil from within as well as without. Where was our (socialist) propaganda now? What part had our ideas held with reality? Where were we? What were we?"

A conference for the purposes of putting a stop to the war was attended by socially committed author Mary Heaton Vorse, Hutchins Hapgood, left wing writer and editor Max Eastman, and a few others. It wound up with a poetry reading, citing the woes of the workers. Later that night, first the I.W.W. poet O'Carroll and then the colony's femme fatale, Polly Holliday, threw themselves into the Bay but were dissuaded from suicide.

That summer the artist *Charles Demuth* (1873–1935) was staying at the Greenwich Village Inn, headquarters for most of the writers. Another guest was the 20-year-old *Stuart Davis* (1894–1964), who was then devoting himself to portraits. When Demuth had been drinking heavily at a party, Davis sometimes took him home, noticing that Demuth was never too drunk to lose interest in his own sensations. Davis was aware, as were a number of others (including the several young women infatuated with "Deem") that Demuth was amorously involved with the strikingly beautiful and aristocratic Helene Lungerieh. He helped her stage a show of Japanese prints. Demuth's loose, painterly views of dunes and boats in the bay (oil and watercolor, and not yet reflecting the influences of Cezanne and Cubism that had affected him in Paris) were shown alongside Stuart Davis's portraits — and perhaps a landscape or two in an exhibition at the Inn.

If a creative momentum was maintained in Provincetown in the summers of 1914 to 1916, the credit goes as much to the Provincetown Players as to the artists, many of whom were their friends and colleagues. So vital and magnetic was the enthusiasm and the imagination they brought to their shared enterprise in the community theater that many (including Marsden Hartley) mistakenly believed that the Players had appeared quite magically in the summer of 1915 when they took over Mary Vorse's fish house and wharf for their theater. Actually, most of the writers and some of the actors were friends who had been spending summers in the town since 1911. Before their Theater on the Wharf, they had written some notable plays and staged them on the Hapgood's porch with sets improvised by Robert Edmond Jones. *Suppressed Desires* by Glaspell and Cook was their first season hit.

The Dunes — Circa 1929 — Photograph courtesy of Cyril Patrick

They were drawn together by a warm camaraderie and by the vision they came to share with George (Jig) Cram Cook of a spontaneous community theater. Cook was an inspiring man who was later to die in Greece. Mary Heaton Vorse described him as "living in the thought of mankind's possibilities." At the core of the group were Cook and his wife, Susan Glaspell. Members of the original group included Hutchins Hapgood and his wife, Neith Boyce; the sculptor William Zorach and his painter wife, Marguerite Zorach, as well as stage designer Robert Edmond Jones and Henry M. Halls, Joe O'Brien, Edward and Stella Ballantine, and Daniel Wilbur Steele and his wife.

In their pre-war years together they had a chance to formulate ideas and develop themes light-heartedly, without being overwhelmed by grim imperatives. Even after 1914 they continued to talk about Freud and Marx, about the suffragettes and Mrs. Parkhurst, about the new art movements that were elbowing out the old, about primitive man, the turkey trot and the new sexual mores. They were writing plays dealing imaginatively with what they thought about and talked about — the very heart and meaning of spontaneous theater.

A new recruit to the group in 1916 was Jack Reed, described by Vorse as a reporter and poet with an immense gusto for living: "He was gay, sanguine, adventurous, lavish in his friendship and his talent and he was a revolutionist." Other additions were blond and beautiful Ann Harding (soon to be a movie star), Louise Bryant, Frederick Burt, poet Harry Kemp with Mary Pyne, Hutch Collins, and the painter, B. J. O. Nordfeldt. The venerable anarchist, Tony Carlin, called by Hapgood "an insatiable searcher after deeper knowledge," brought with him a young friend with whom he was sharing a fish house, Eugene O'Neill, who shyly admitted he had written some plays and sat in the next room while they read his *Bound East for Cardiff.*

Susan Glaspell described the night the O'Neill play opened on the wharf: "There was a fog just as the script demanded. A fog bell in the harbor. The tide was in and it washed under us and around . . . of the 19 plays put on that summer, six were by O'Neill."

A witty take-off on the stormy loves of Jack Reed and Mabel Dodge was *Constancy,* a play by Neith Hapgood. In 1916 the artistically voracious socialite, Mabel Dodge, arrived at the Cape with her new love interest, Maurice Sterne, a robust darkly handsome, Russian-born artist whose presence Mabel associated with primitive passions (perhaps because of the acclaimed series he had painted on the Island of Bali, a success she kept prodding him to repeat by furnishing him with unusual settings). After traveling the Cape together and consummating their relationship at an inn — for the sake of art — she found a studio in the dunes for Maurice (the abandoned Coast Guard Station at Peak Hill where O'Neill had worked), handily separated from the house she would maintain on the opposite Bay side for herself and her very sophisticated entourage.

A house guest of Jack Reed and an intimate of the Players was *Marsden Hartley* (1877–1943), a friend and admirer of Charles Demuth — they had known each other in Paris in 1912 when both moved in the circle of American expatriates around Gertrude Stein. Each had experienced in his own way the electric shock of Cubism and Cezanne. In Germany the following year Hartley had been influenced by the Blue Rider group of Munich led by Wassily Kandinsky, the foremost advocate of abstract painting in Europe, and exhibited at Der Sturm in Berlin. Returning to Germany in 1914, Hartley reacted to the military atmosphere by turning out a series of large, rhythmically pulsating compositions based on the shapes of the iron cross and other emblems. With their strong colors, flatly-banded and checkered patterns, they bridged a gap between Cubism and Expressionism. Back in the U.S. he turned to pastel colors and to the most severely structured abstractions of his career, often reduced to a sparse confrontation of circles and triangles. Some that he did in Provincetown were called "movements."

Charles Demuth
"After Sir Christopher Wren"
oil on canvas
Worcester Art Museum, Worcester, Massachusetts

36

In the summer of 1915 Demuth was in Provincetown with Edward Fisk, a handsome American painter he had met in Paris (Fisk later married the sister of Agnes O'Neill and went West). Looking back on those months Hartley saw it as a time of intense work, intense play, filled with satisfactions. In spite of Demuth's poor health (he was not yet a diabetic but he had trouble with a hip and had to walk with a cane), he insisted on being included in the players' strenuous activities. That summer he had an acting part in Mary Heaton Vorse's *A Girl on the Wharf.* No party was too debilitating, no nocturnal revel too outlandish to be remembered in a drawing or watercolor.

Demuth never made a secret of his admiration for Aubrey Beardsley. Because of his own dandified elegance and aloofness, and the combination of delicacy with perversity in his work, it was easy to suggest — as Hartley himself did — that Demuth was perpetuating the *fin de siecle* malaise. In Paris around 1920 Demuth learned that he was a diabetic and presumably doomed. But he was one of the first to be treated with the new drug, insulin; it sustained his life for a decade and a half. Toward the end of his life Demuth experimented periodically and not very successfully with erotic drawings. If only dimly they illuminate some of the tensions and fantasy escapes of the war years.

In Provincetown in the mid- and later teens Demuth was occupied with the series of watercolor illustrations of Henry James' *Turn of the Screw,* a task he had undertaken for his own pleasure (not initially for a publisher), and also with a series of drawings of precariously balancing acrobats. In both, blotted washes flow in and through the deftly meandering pencil lines.

Demuth was not the only painter in Provincetown to be attracted by the classical proportions and tower of the Methodist Church. But despite his long-cherished interest in architecture, he evidently postponed the challenge to paint it until, stylistically, he could "make it his own," equating its mathematically-derived arcs and angles to the geometry of Cubism. He was ready to tackle it in the summer of 1919, not in oils or watercolor, but in the newly-adopted medium of tempera which enabled him to treat the architectural forms of the tower with greater precision. But as Demuth had shown in his acrobats, he felt the need of an active, tenuous equilibrium. For this he borrowed certain devices from the Futurists: by extending the arcs and angles of solid forms into surrounding space he agitated the classic stability. He then further heightened this dynamism by filling the space above with crisscrossing shafts that resemble searchlights raking the sky.

During Demuth's summers in Provincetown, the colony was treated to an example of an exceptional artist who had managed to "have his (abstract) cake and eat it (realistically) too." Moreover, he was able to combine realism and abstraction so lightheartedly, with so much delicacy and wit that the synthesis seldom seemed labored or pedantic. Flowers and fish, acrobats and architecture emerge from an impeccable structure of planes with most of their tangible clues intact. In a surprising prismatic sequence we discover wooden steps, perhaps those leading up to Days' studios. If much of his work fell within the province of the Precisionists, Demuth sidestepped the confines of a puritanical repressiveness, which gave that group the nickname the "Immaculates." For Demuth, life experience was too varied, strange, bitter, sensuous and contradictory to be sterilized.

Organizations Launched

By 1914 the sheer numbers of artists in the community gave some urgency to the forming of an organization for the purpose of exhibiting their work as well as for the exchange of ideas. The founding of the Provincetown Art Association took place on August 22 of that summer. By the second year, there were 147

Provincetown skyline with Methodist Church — Photograph courtesy of Cyril Patrick

members. A president, banker William H. Young, was elected, and officers. The vice-presidents included Charles Webster Hawthorne and E. Ambrose Webster, heads of the two leading schools, along with the venerable William F. Halsall, a marine painter who had served in the Union Navy in the Civil War. Their first exhibition was held in the summer of 1915 at Town Hall.

The Greenwich Village contingent was not the only one that cherished memories of Paris cafe life: Hawthorne and his expatriate friends had also enjoyed the carefree nights of excited talk, banter and jokes at the Cafe du Dome and the Rotonde where the wine flowed until morning. Perhaps in the hope of creating a surrogate atmosphere, with a good bit of the all-American stag party thrown in, they founded the Beachcombers as a member's club for professionals in the arts, music and theater in the summer of 1916, finding it a waterfront headquarters not far from where the Art Association would have its museum. There were games and other activities — chess, costume affairs, minstrel shows and all kinds of entertainment — to raise money for worthy causes (in 1916 they raised an impressive sum for relief of those widowed and orphaned by a storm at sea that year). Once a year there was the "Combers" clambake with George Elmer Browne in his white linen hat playing a prominent role. But the weekly Friday night gathering supplied the escape valve after a hard working day in the studio. On nights when John Noble was there highjinks were to be expected, and by previous arrangement between the police and Mrs. Noble, he was to be safely stowed away in jail after a certain hour in the morning. Stories about the gaiety of Beachcombers' evenings filled outsiders with envy: it is said that the universally popular fisherman, Manny Zora, became an actor with the Players in order to qualify for membership in the "Combers."

In 1920 the wharf and fish house that had served as a theater for the Provincetown Players (near the East end of Commercial Street) was converted into a nocturnal coffee shop or alcohol-less night club called "The Sixes and Sevens." This was launched by six lively, enterprising art students recently discharged from war-time service: Courtney Allen, Jerry Farnsworth, Reeves Euler (Eddie), Vollian Rann, Patrick Finley and Walter Hayn; each could perform on a musical instrument to furnish entertainment and Hayn was also a lusty vocalist. Dressed in open-neck shirts, sailor's trousers and white aprons, they served ice cream, sandwiches, tea and coffee for prices in pennies and nickels, and there was a cover charge of eleven cents. From eight o'clock the wharf was filled with artists, students, theater people, and a sprinkling of vacationists who supped and danced on the old plank floor until the last bus came down Commercial at eleven and honked for the late patrons. "The Sixes and Sevens" was a great success during the summers of 1920 and 1921; it came to an end only because the fish house burned down late that year. Most of its live-wire proprietors became well-known artists and permanent members of the colony; Reeves Euler became a year-round resident.

The 1920's: The Young Lions

In the autumn Charles Hawthorne left for his home and studio in New York and most of the students returned to the hinterlands. Remaining in Provincetown during the twenties and lending continuity to the colony, were *Edwin Dickinson* (1891–   ), *Ross Moffett* (1888–1971) and *Karl Knaths* (1891–1971). All in their early thirties, they were, in a phrase that Josephine Del Deo applied to Moffett, "the young lions" of the colony. Dickinson and Moffett, close friends since their studies with Hawthorne before the war, had returned after wartime service confident that Provincetown offered a chance to develop independently without the pressures of big city living. Knaths was even more wary of urban centers, whether in American or Europe, than his friend Ross Moffett whom he had known as a fellow student in Chicago.

With few other artist companions around, they were drawn together, especially in explorations of the Cape. When Knaths would rail at the hold of Hawthorne and his colleagues on the newly-housed Art Association, Moffett was there to act as mediator. During the years when the Art Association was split between traditional and modern factions, Moffett usually identified himself with the moderns for whom Knaths was a champion. Dickinson, a close friend of Hawthorne's, ordinarily served on traditional juries but on occasion crossed over to the other side.

Their commitment to a life close to nature had nothing to do with production of sentimental views: the approach was based on a total aesthetic philosophy. For Knaths nature was to be apprehended through the insights of occultism, religion, and the structures of Cezanne and the Cubists; for Moffett the lure first of impressionism then of abstraction was deflected by his Tolstoyan humanism. The imagination of Dickinson would be shaped to neither a traditional nor a modern mold. In his on-the-spot landscapes there is obvious sensuous relish in what the eye can see — the sweep of silvery light registered in nuances of tone — but even there, he enjoys certain mysteries, enigmatic dislocations of reality.

Born in Seneca Falls in 1891, Edwin Dickinson grew up in the Finger Lakes region of upstate New York, the son of a minister. When he came to Provincetown in 1911 to study with Hawthorne, he had already worked under William Merritt Chase at the Art Students League. In his opinion Chase was "a famous and beautiful demonstrator," and a fine teacher, but he was surpassed by Hawthorne whom Dickinson said was "above reproach."

In 1914 when Dickinson was a handsome fellow with a debonair moustache he painted a self-portrait with most of his head submerged in murky shadow and only one eye distinctly defined. "Hawthorne liked that one," he said. Although Dickinson's style diverged from Hawthorne's on the one hand by its greater romanticism and on the other by its greater precision, they remained lifelong friends. This early self-portrait was followed over the years by a remarkable series in which his elegant square-cut beard is as distinctive as the piercing grey-blue eyes. Often the features are in shadow and the head oddly juxtaposed with paraphernalia: once a Civil War cap, and in one of his masterpieces now owned by the National Academy of Design a geometric chart emblematic of Dickinson's passion for perspective.

After Naval service during World War I as radio operator on the Nantucket Lightship, he traveled and studied on his own in Europe, returning with an affecting memory of El Greco's *Burial of the Count d'Orgaz* in Toledo. Years later he told Elaine de Kooning: "(After seeing it) I knew where my aspirations lay." He set to work happily, eating, sleeping and painting in one of the rough and ready studios then available for fifty dollars a year in a group built over Days lumber yard. After weatherproofing the floor with old tacked-down canvases he felt he was better off than most, and settled in for one of the seventeen winters he was to spend in Provincetown before moving to Wellfleet. In all seasons he rowed and sailed; he took arduous walks across the dunes to the "back shore," sometimes before dawn, occasionally in the buff, less frequently in a raging storm when there was a wreck. He joined Moffett and Knaths on hikes upcape to Wellfleet and back after a meal with the men at the Coast Guard, who were always hospitable.

There may well have been times when there were gala gatherings of artists, young people, models, and musicians with fishermen and other town types but the intriguing company assembled in his large painting of 1929 called *Anniversary* were never together in a real party. The central figure, Coast Guard veteran Ben Atkins (a favorite model of his and Moffett's), was painted alone from life in Dickinson's studio, as were all the other characters posed for, one by one, by friends. The ensemble, with its curious sense of timelessness, existed only in his imagination. Speaking of an earlier work, *The Cello Player,* he said: "After the piece was about 50 sittings along I decided to show the cellist to be in a bowl comprised of the floor and the objects on it. ... The time given to the piece was, of course, several times greater than the 870 hours execution sittings."

The problem of creating tangible, though ambiguously related, figures and objects in a fantasied space was to occupy him on single capital works for years at a time, and during a period when he was getting very little attention from critics or galleries. He was too difficult to classify: the exquisite and palpable realism of his figures and still life qualified him for a niche as a traditionalist, but he was as disquieting as a surrealist in the strangely juxtaposed forms of his imaginative compositions, with their oddly tilting planes and mysterious light. But Dickinson would not be discouraged or hurried. In 1927 he was already at work on one of his first epic works, *The Fossil Hunters* (acquired in 1955 by the Whitney), with the figure of Barbara Brown Malicoat — her luxuriant hair cascading down — scraped out and painted in different positions several times that winter. Modeling for another figure was his sister Antoinette (Tibi), who was keeping house for Dickinson at the time. The picture was awarded the second Altman Prize by the National Academy of Design in 1929.

In 1928 he married Frances Foley, a young artist and teacher whose deep interest in classical archaeology was to initiate their travels in Greece many years later. After years of living in the studio building on Pearl Street, they bought an old house in 1939 on the moors in Wellfleet. After the mid forties, as they began spending the winters in New York, Dickinson was increasingly taking his place in the larger art world both as a painter and as a teacher. He taught, he said, first for love, secondly for money; in posts (among others) at Wellesley, Cooper Union and The Art Students League in New York, the Art School of the Brooklyn Museum and at Pratt Institute in Brooklyn. He was a most loved and sought-after teacher.

In 1943 his *Composition with Still Life,* a capital work of 1933–37, was chosen by the Museum of Modern Art for its exhibition of "Romantic Painting in America" and later added to the collection. In 1952 Dickinson was selected as one of the Fifteen Americans in the Museum's prestigious series on native artists.

In 1952, *Art News* devoted an article to his epic painting (nine years in the making), *Ruin at Daphne,* inspired by one of his winter sojourns in Greece but partly painted in Truro. Greece with its subterranean levels of civilization, amplified his concept of life and nature as many-layered, and the excavation subject invited an extension of the linear perspectives that continued to fascinate him. In spite of its meticulously painted colonnades and stratifications, the picture (since 1955 in the collection of the Metropolitan Musuem in New York) is curiously abstract.

It was not until the work of the Abstract Expressionists gained currency that certain distortions and elisions in Dickinson's paintings could be better undorotood. And ho had a romarkablo rapport with tho radioal now otyloo. At tho Museum of Modern Art he once led me through a special exhibition of the black paintings of Ad Reinhardt explaining how very adroit the artist had been in producing these close-toned works.

On the occasion of the 1976 retrospective exhibition of his work presented by the Provincetown Art Association, his old friends and former students recounted his qualities and endearing idiosyncracies. Fellow artist Bruce McKain who had posed for a week in 1932 in uniform, as a sleeping soldier in a nocturnal Civil War scene, recalled seeing the figure and surroundings all scraped out, leaving only the heavy shoes he had worn for the part. Dickinson had said, "I think the only good thing is the pair of shoes." The shoes remained to become part of a different composition (McKain did not know its title or location). But odd juxtapositions were not unusual in Dickinson's more romantic subjects. Barbara Malicoat cited another instance: "A critic asked why he used a rose, a plough, a figure, part of a stove, in a single canvas. Dick said that if all these elements were painted honestly, solidly, then they all belonged."

It is the cloudy day on the Cape when hills and dunes are so softened by mist, that most often tempts Dickinson to set up his easel and launch into a small landscape that can be captured in an hour or two by, in his favorite phrase, *"premier coup."* Painted broadly but with a fine discrimination of nuances of chalky or greyed tones, these works suppress most details, emphasize a total image which can be subtly enigmatic.

In the pure whites and spare silvery tones of his pencil and charcoal drawings, Dickinson is less romantic. Softly fluid spaces weave through and around forms defined with linear precision. He often surprises the viewer by an odd angle of vision: a mere glimpse of landscape framed by window mullions; the lucid geometry of a spiral staircase seen from below. Of a chair that he painted upside down he said, "This is not a chair for sitting in, it is a chair for painting."

In Wellfleet in 1967 Dickinson showed me a canvas, *South Wellfleet Inn,* 1950, that he said he regarded as one of his most important works. At first glance it looked, deceptively, like a Cubist painting; at the same time it seemed to project a Surrealist's questioning of the nature of reality. After decades of explorations with perspective, he had pulled off a stunning *tour de force* in which perspective was exactly reversed. At the top of the picture the gables and dormers of the inn are seen as if from below. Cutting off the view of most of the building, but juxtaposed so that it seems a continuation of the structure, is the artist's canvas. In his painting, the inn's facade is repeated seven times through tilting angles, with each rendering diminishing in size and clarity as it careens toward the viewer into final nothingness. Explanations as to conscious or unconscious symbolism are never supplied by Edwin Dickinson.

Artist-philosopher, humanist, historian, something of a scientist, delving into the archaeology of the Cape End — these "hats" were all worn by *Ross Moffett* in his fifty-eight years in Provincetown. Edwin Dickinson once said that Moffett was much more Provincetown than Hawthorne. When Moffett wrote his indispensable *Art in Narrow Streets* on the first 33 years of the Provincetown Art Association, he was modest about his own role that was in fact so central. Born into a family of farmers in Clearwater, Iowa, in 1888, Moffett made his way to the Chicago Art Institute for three years of study, then to Provincetown shortly after he had seen the revolutionary Armory Show at the Institute. The conflict in his own work between traditionalist and modern, made him a sympathetic and effective interpreter of each faction to the other. The strains between the opposing coteries might have overwhelmed the Association without his mediation.

With his gravity and earnestness, his soft-spoken and extremely polite manner, young Moffett was anything but a bohemian, yet tough-mindedness, candour and restrained high spirits are also marked in his 1915 *Self-Portrait*. He became adept, as this portrait shows, in working with the strongly contrasted lights and shadows and coloristic method taught by Hawthorne. But shortly after it was painted, he was haunted by doubts as to whether this technique was right for him. Almost overnight in 1916, he reversed direction and arrived at his own style of muted colors and flamboyant contours; in a series of rather large paintings that might be called "folk tableaux," the figures and the town environment were treated about equally as inseparable components. Contours in both assume a rhythmic emphasis that moves the eye from one group to another along perspectives where the harbor is either glimpsed or implied.

If Hawthorne's Portuguese were cast after Mediterranean archetypes, Moffett's, at this stage, assumed a kind of Gothic animation and sometimes a

Breughelesque humor. He relished the contrasts and occasional outlandishness of patriarchs, moppets, gossips. In these early works, the Portuguese are not idealized, nor are they symbols; there is an understated sympathy with people who must endure bleakness and waiting. His *The Old Fisherman* of 1918 won three awards including the first Julius Hallgarten Prize at the National Academy.

Following a stint in the Army, Moffett married Dorothy Lake Gregory in 1920, also a fledgling artist; she had studied with Hawthorne in 1915 after earlier work under Robert Henri. After a decision to live year round in Provincetown, they set up twin studios in the immense space of an old shirt factory on Court Street heated only by a laundry stove. In the decade of the 1920's when Moffett was influenced by Cezanne, he was concerned with geometric elements in opposition. In 1930 at a time when his reputation as an innovating modern was at its height, he was selected to serve on the jury of the Carnegie International along with Henri Matisse.

The flattened shapes and spaces of modernism nevertheless often frustrated a yearning to deal with certain concepts of humanity derived early in life from, among others, Tolstoy. His search for a symbolic expression based on the human figure led him back to the example of Masaccio whose paintings and frescoes he had studied in Florence on an extended post-wedding trip in 1923. The more ample, idealized figures of working men and women he derived from Renaissance examples served him well in the WPA murals he painted in the depression years for the post offices of Holyoke, Revere and Somerville and for the Town Hall and High School in Provincetown.

The National Academy elected Ross Moffett a full member in 1942. Twelve years later, when he was entering his seventies, the Academy commissioned him, along with Louis Bouche, to paint murals based on the former President's life at the Eisenhower Memorial Museum in Abilene, Kansas. But he took the greatest satisfaction in his success in a different kind of enterprise: the saving of 1400 acres of the Province Lands which, largely through his efforts (begun in 1959), were incorporated into the National Seashore.

Moffett had an engrossing interest in the archaeology and ecology of the Cape End; he studied and excavated ancient Indian sites and wrote about them for publication with scientific precision.

In 1970, although he had been in treatment for cancer since 1963, he served as artist in residence for the Fine Arts Work Center, then in its third season. He died March 13, 1971.

An inlander, *Karl Knaths* found his way to Provincetown by the sea unerringly, as if by some clear destiny. Having put down roots, he was not often to leave the tree-guarded house near the very end of the land. His friends dreamed of Europe — even Dickinson and Moffett had sojourned abroad — but Knaths never wanted to leave American shores. The painting style he had derived indirectly from Europeans (Cezanne and the Cubists) was something universal, offering the right means for the expression of the nature around him — the America of Johnny Appleseed and Thoreau.

He was called Otto when he was growing up in the still somewhat rural Wisconsin community of Portage (he was born in Eau Claire). His family was of German descent and ran a bakery. His teen-age decision to study art took him to the Chicago Art Institute where one of his fellow students was Ross Moffett, who was already talking of Provincetown, where living was cheap. Thoreau, whose writings on the Cape he devoured, had also convinced Knaths that "you could do what you wanted to do."

He came to Provincetown in 1919, taking a studio the earlier tenants of which had been Eugene O'Neill and Charles Demuth. Later he rented a sail-loft for thirty dollars annually, making it habitable with salvaged lumber and an abandoned stove. Before dawn he was listening to the sound of oarlocks as the

Towne Crier, Commercial Street — Circa 1920 — Photograph courtesy of Cyril Patrick

men of the fleet rowed to their schooners. The fishermen were to be his subjects —not as models summoned to his studio, but as a part of the maritime nature that challenged him most.

His drive to transpose a subject into simplified planes developed gradually in the years following his first exposure to modern art when the famous Armory Show traveled to the Chicago Art Institute; initially he had been moved by the Van Goghs and the Cezannes he had seen there. In Provincetown, Knaths' paintings with their emphasis on structure, attracted the attention of a mentor, Agnes Weinirch, who was at the center of a group of young rebels more sophisticated in abstraction than Knaths. Weinrich had studied in Paris with the Cubists (probably Albert Gleizes); she and her coterie had pored over books on numerical theory by Gleizes and Gino Severini. As he was accepted into this group, Knaths (he now called himself "Karl") found that his work, like theirs, was not in high regard with the "old hats" of the Art Association. He has admitted that in these years he was "a scrapper."

After his marriage in 1924 to Helen Weinrich, a pianist and sister of Agnes, Knaths acquired an acre of land set back in trees at the extreme West End and began, with wood from a just-demolished parsonage, to build a house for the three of them. Not far from the Atlantic just around the bend, affording glimpses of the Bay, but close to marshes, woods, and moors, it was the perfect spot for an artist based on themes in nature, not panoramic landscapes or picturesque vistas, but places teeming with creature life.

From his reading of the Bible and the transcendental philosophers, from the mystical doctrines of Emmanual Swedenborg and the spatial theories of Gleizes, Knaths gradually derived a concept of a structured universe to which the structures of a painting could be related. Every experience in the studio or on his long daily walks—they were continued until he was in his seventies—was fitted logically into this framework of his thought.

In his mature work, Knaths continued to determine the spatial divisions of a canvas by the "golden section," ardently pursued by many of the young moderns in the 1920's, also incorporating theories of dynamic symmetry from Jay Hambridge, author of "The Elements of Dynamic Symmetry." For him numbers like the magical number seven, could also have a mystical meaning. As an additional means of insuring ordered relationships, Knaths drew on music: often both the spatial divisions and range of color in a painting were matched to the harmonic progression of tones in a musical composition. Yet in his imagination all this structuring had to be kept fluid and allowed to develop associational meanings.

Knaths kept a large drawer in a studio table that was a surprising feast of color: dozens of clam shells generously filled with oil paints in subtly modulated range of hues; invariably they had been selected from the intricate charts of the Ostwald color system. For each new painting he would mix a new clam shell palette, a new set of variations chosen from the more than 900 established by the color scientist. Through a miracle of imaginative juggling, both of spatial proportions and colors, he preserved a relationship with the forms in nature that had inspired the painting in the beginning and that would emerge from the color planes as he worked.

Knaths summed up the logic of his intricate method in simple terms: "In time I came to approach the motif in reverse...from the canvas to nature and not from nature to the canvas." He added: "When the composition remains abstract I always feel a certain need for a meaning. I like to see a shape or a measure of color that is beautiful in itself take on the character and meaning of a natural object."

45

The collector, Duncan Phillips, bought an abstracted *Geranium* from Knaths in 1926 and later steadily acquired other works for the Phillips Gallery in Washington, D.C. From 1938 to 1950 Knaths spent some weeks in Washington as an artist-in-residence at the gallery.

During the depression years Richard Miller, director of the local WPA projects, was prevailed upon to put Knaths to work at Town Hall renovating old stage scenery. For the Provincetown High School he painted a mural on the history of musical instruments; he was employed for two years painting murals on the history of music for the Falmouth High School.

The influx of abstract artists in the post-war years brought new stimulation and companionship. He happily shared the tasks of Forum '49 with the Abstract Expressionists. Hans Hofmann was already a respected colleague; they exchanged visits almost ceremoniously once a year.

Knaths worked productively until the end of his life (his work handled in New York by the Paul Rosenberg Gallery). He never hesitated about shifting from more to less abstract, never far from nature. Occasionally his thinking about man and his destiny, or his reading (which continually ranged from science to mysticism) would lead to a more symbolic expression. In a masterpiece now in the Albright-Knox Art Gallery, *Zero Adam I,* his speculations about the atom led him to an image of Adam in the guise of a fisherman toiling under a sun that is at the same time the spinning atom.

Knaths died after a short illness in 1971. Jack Tworkov, a neighbor who first met Knaths in 1924, said: "Until the mid forties [Knaths was] the most advanced painter in the country with a modern view, just as Dickinson was the best and most distinguished following a more traditional path."

The 1920's: The Art Association — A House Divided

On July 4th, 1921, the seventh annual exhibition of the Provincetown Art Association opened in its new home, a stately white colonial-style building of fine proportions pleasantly set off from surroundings on Commercial Street (at Bangs) by shade trees and a lawn. The classic and serene appearance of the restored mansion belied the stormy but vital future that lay ahead of its new tenants.

Founded in 1914, the Association held its first exhibition the following year in the north room of Town Hall: its annual shows were subsequently held there or in other borrowed facilities. Beginning with 147 members, by 1917 it had 289. As has been previously noted, the first president (traditionally not an artist) was William H. Young. The important posts of vice-presidents, who set policy in art matters, included the two heads of schools, Charles W. Hawthorne and Ambrose Webster, as well as the marine painter William F. Halsall, a long time resident.

Even during those early homeless years, the annual exhibitions attracted some outstanding artists, among them: satirist Peggy Bacon; Bror Nordfeldt, who was exploring new techniques in printmaking; the well-known etcher, W. H. W. Bicknell; pioneering local abstractionist, Blanche Lazzell; Charles Demuth, an internationally-seasoned modern; fledgling cubist, Karl Knaths, along with the local recorder of town landscape, Nancy Ferguson.

As the Association was taking possession of its new quarters in 1921, the task of drawing up a constitution and by-laws was given to Charles Hawthorne with his friends, Max Bohm, George Elmer Browne, John Noble, and Dr. Percival Eaton. The rules for election of officers then drawn up tended to render the Art Association almost a closed body. Eight of the twelve trustees elected in 1921 were still in office seven years later; during that same time there was only one change in the board of honorary vice-presidents. The result was that although the work of some of the moderns did appear in exhibitions, it was judged by a jury not sympathetic to their intention; all out moderns did not become trustees or honorary vice-presidents. Presented to a meeting on June 17, 1926, was a petition drawn up on Ross Moffett and Tod Lindenmuth and signed by thirty members, asking that four painters of modernistic sympathies be added to the jury for the forthcoming exhibition. They said: "Considering the fact that there are in Provincetown two groups, each having a different opinion as to what forms of painting are most likely to manifest genuine artistic merit, we regard it as unfair and out of keeping with American traditions for representatives of either group to be the sole arbiters as to what paintings shall be shown in the galleries of the Association." At a meeting one month later, a motion setting up a separate exhibition of works of the modern group was passed.

The "First Modernistic Exhibition" opened the following year on July 2, presenting 75 oils and 51 prints, drawings, and watercolors and three wood carvings, all very carefully selected by the "modern" jury of Floyd Clymer, Edwin Dickinson, Charles A. Kaeselau, Karl Knaths, Blanche Lazzell, Lucy L'Engle, Tod Lindenmuth, Dorothy Loeb, Ellen Ravenscroft, Agnes Weinrich and Ross Moffett. Among those who showed for the first time were Niles Spencer, Jack Tworkov, George Ault and Charles Martin, who also gave a lecture on modern art. Under the sponsorship of Teachers College, Columbia, he taught summer art classes in Provincetown.

As recalled by Ross Moffett, historian of the Provincetown Art Asssociation (in *Art in Narrow Streets*), the characteristic shared by most exhibitors in the new modern show was a concern with composition, the "deliberately organized or structural base," usually absent in academic paintings. With the possible exception of Blanche Lazzell, an early non-objective artist, most canvases retained somewhat recognizable imagery with a predominant influence from Cezanne and from early Picasso and Braque.

As artists turned away from the representation of familiar appearances they found a new security in the realm of mathematically determined proportions. Among the year-round residents this was stimulated by the appearance in Provincetown of a book on the aesthetic of compass and number, *Du Cubisme au Classicisme* (originally published in Paris in 1921) by the Futurist painter, Gino Severini. Translated chapter by chapter and passed from hand to hand, it inspired a fever of geometric inspection of masterpieces from all cultures in hope of discovering the mathematical formula for perfect proportion. This was further stimulated by a lecture on the subject given in 1932 by Ambrose Webster, Provincetown's earliest modern. A strong impression was made by a paragraph, quoted in the front of the 1935 modern exhibition catalog: "The outstanding principle is the use of ratios as found in geometry, which bring about eurythmic relationships between the parts of the picture. Following this principle, the artist must be free to bend the line, change the pattern, to create new forms which may not be found in nature." The geometric explorations of the moderns were thought to supersede an earlier mathematically-based system of proportions promoted by Jay Hambridge and others in books on "dynamic symmetry." Since this formula, widely discussed in Provincetown in the late 1920's, was usually applied to representational works, it had enlisted the interest of painters working in a variety of styles. It enjoyed a comeback in 1933 when two lectures were given by Hambridge disciple, Julian Bowles.

With the impact of the Depression, stylistic differences seemed less important. After several years of peaceful coexistence, in August, 1936, the trustees voted for a combined show of moderns and conservatives for the following year, and at the same time provided for new appointments that would make the board of honorary vice-presidents more liberal in outlook. Each group was to have equal hanging space and the two-jury system was maintained.

The first combined exhibition, opening in July, 1937, attracted critics from Boston and New York. Their near-unanimous judgment was that the moderns and the conservatives looked much alike. The New York critic, Edward Alden Jewel, mistook the conservative wall for the modern. Dorothy Adlow of the *Christian Science Monitor* noted that "modernistic" ideas had percolated through. "More and more does conservatism and liberalism seem a state of mind in the individual artist, and less a matter of technical leanings." In reviewing these opinions Ross Moffett found only one negative reaction, from the *Boston Globe* reviewer, who found Loren MacIver's picture childish and silly.

The Changing Scene in the 1930's and 1940's

In the summers of 1928 and 1929 *Raphael Soyer* (1899–   ) lived in a shack on the Provincetown waterfront. But when he went sketching, he resolutely turned his back on the picturesque harbor vistas; working instead from various spots on the unpaved Bradford Street. In a departure from the thronged thoroughfares for which he was to become best known, he drew and later painted deserted, low-keyed townscapes like the somber *Railroad Yard* with its sweep of a back street lot paralleling the railroad tracks and held in tension by the distant gables of Town Hall. In the deliberate tough-mindedness and understatement of such a subject (in contrast to the usual response to the town's quaintness or its natural setting), Soyer was forecasting an attitude that was to grow in the 1930's, especially after the Depression when American Scene painting came to be associated more with what reflected the changing patterns of society than with the eternal and relatively unchanging nature that had fascinated earlier Provincetown artists.

The most stunning challenge to romanticized landscape painting came from *Edward Hopper* (1882–1967), a permanent half-year resident of the Cape Tip after 1930 when he built a steep roofed house and studio in Truro, carpentered to his own design. Starkly situated atop a bare hill, it was a place to live and paint for six months of the year for himself and his wife for the rest of their lives. Tall, serious, known for his stubborn silences, at 42 he was winning long-delayed recognition for his usually bleak, tersely simplified, hauntingly-lighted New York scenes.

In earlier years Hopper had painted at Cape Elizabeth and Gloucester. He considered the Cape landscape somewhat "too soft," but liked its brilliant light that stripped white buildings down to a bare geometry while accentuating the particulars of doorways and shutters. In his second Truro summer, Hopper painted the majestic, unpeopled landscape, Camel's Hump, but the nature he usually sought out in painting was lived-in countryside — nature stubbornly maintaining a presence in the face of the ruinous inroads of commerce.

He sketched from his car, finding subjects more often bordering on the highways than along the picturesque dirt roads and beaches. His haunting *Cape Cod Evening,* of 1939, is an example of his search for the correct documentation of details so essential to his realism. Writing from his Cape studio of the picture (now in the collection of the Whitney Museum), he noted: "It is no exact transcription of a place but pieced together from sketches and mental impressions of things in the vicinity. The grove of locust trees was done from sketches of trees nearby. The doorway of the house came from Orleans almost two miles from here. The figures were done almost entirely without models and the dry, blowing grasses can be seen from my studio window in the late summer or autumn. In the woman I am trying to get the broad, strong-jawed face and blond hair of a Finnish type of which there are many on Cape Cod. The man is a dark-haired Yankee. The dog is listening to something, probably a whippoorwill or some evening sound."

For his painting of the *Methodist Church,* now the Provincetown Heritage Museum (formerly the Chrysler Museum), Hopper set aside his usual ironical emphasis on incongruous elements in American architecture. The painting reflects instead his satisfaction in the structural solidity and light-reflecting quality of rooftops pyramiding up to the tower.

Hopper saw Provincetown as a transposed outpost of the urban environment. By then, the clapboard houses along traffic-jammed streets (many built in the 19th century and some earlier) conveyed by their converted aspects, a loss of roots and the transiency of a vacation spot. At the junction of Bradford and Johnson Streets, he found a prime motif in a rambling, many-gabled rooming house that was once a mansion. Its lavish awnings signal a lingering pretension to gentility while its curtailed lawn with glaring sign announcing overnight accommodations, proclaim its fallen estate. Hopper sketched it from his car, returning several evenings (while the proprietor grew alarmed) to record every detail of its full night-time illumination. The result was the unforgettable image of *Rooms for Tourists* (collection of Yale Art Gallery, New Haven, Connecticut).

From the late 1920's until the beginning of World War II, *Loren MacIver* (1909–   ) lived year-round in the dunes overlooking the Atlantic. In a spot near the abandoned Peaked Hill Coast Guard Station that had been the home of Eugene O'Neill, she and her poet-husband, Lloyd Frankenberg, built a durable shack from driftwood. The only access from town was via an extremely arduous walk through the rugged dunes; the isolation they sought was almost complete.

She liked to have a pot of coffee ready for the lone coast guardsman who patrolled the beach each night with his flashlight. Sometimes the crew of a friendly fishing boat would pick them up at four in the morning to join their seine fishing.

MacIver had developed abstraction in a personal and poetic vein in which images and symbols were subtly identified with fragments of reality. The effect of sweeping horizons around her in the dunes was to focus her attention all the more on small tangible discoveries that sparked inward associations; a nest of tern's eggs, or cranberries in winter. Her painting of *The Shack* (owned by the Museum of Modern Art), laid out flatly in a cruciform shape so that interior and exterior are seen at once, makes a pattern of shelves, wood-burning stove, kerosene lamps. Softly surrounded by an oval of dune grasses, it seems a metaphor for her personal womb-like sense of enclosure in the midst of the vastness of nature.

Frederick Waugh (1861–1940), a virtuoso of marine subjects, had spent 15 years abroad painting on the Isle of Sark, at St. Ives, and other celebrated coastal spots before coming to Provincetown in 1928. From his vast studio in the West End he could not see the Atlantic or even the Bay, but he said he missed only the rocks. He was able to continue to paint crashing ocean surf from remembered details of the early years when he had painted on the spot.

Waugh bought a 200-year-old colonial home at Commercial and Nickerson Streets in the West End, owned by a sea captain who made a fortune in the slave trade. For a studio addition, great planks were dragged there from an ancient wreck, and a massive balcony constructed over the fireplace completed the maritime effect with ships' lanterns suspended from davits.

Waugh was well-able to afford this lavish construction: he was unable to satisfy his dealer's demand for his large paintings of seacoast subjects. They sold in a range from $500 to $2,000 and his annual income from paintings was said to be about $30,000. The immense popularity of his marines was sustained season after season. In fact he won the popularity prize at the Carnegie International Exhibition in Pittsburgh for five years in succession: for *Tropic Seas* in 1934, for

©Arnold Newman

Edward Hopper & Jo N. Hopper — 1960, Truro, Massachusetts.
Photograph by Arnold Newman

50

Ante Meridian in 1935, for *Big Water* in 1936, *Meridian* in 1937, and for *Pounding Surf* in 1938.

Waugh worked best to the tumultuous crescendos of Beethoven and Sibelius. In a typical subject, the rock-coursing surf was seen almost at eye-level with a luminous wave or two looming above, the ensemble framed by a glimpse of rugged coast.

A shy, pleasant man with an interest in many aspects of paintings, Waugh felt boxed in by the accolades constantly given to his sea subjects. In a second studio further along Commercial Street (this one with a view of the Bay), he painted his "hobby" pictures, ranging from still-lifes which he invested with a vein of whimsical fantasy to near-abstractions. But his efforts to explore modern idioms invariably met with indifference. His home and the nearby homes and studios of his family were sometimes dubbed "Waughsville." His son, Coulton Waugh, was also a marine painter but, unlike his father, he included ships on his seas. He lived with his wife in Provincetown's oldest house, at 72 Commercial Street, where he ran a ship model shop. Opposite this house on a wharf was the costume shop run by Frederick's daughter, Gwenth. Floyd Clymer, Waugh's son-in-law, developed a spirited personal style with modern simplifications in which he also sometimes painted the sea or the bay but with broad, flattened areas of color. Helen Sawyer writes: "Floyd Clymer and Coulton were, of course, a part of our group at the Waughs' where we went every Sunday evening for music and chess." They were also often joined there by Edwin Dickinson, an ardent chess player.

Helen Sawyer (1900–   ), daughter of the artist Wells Sawyer, had come to Provincetown when she was fourteen to study with Hawthorne. There she met John "Bill" Noble. She said: "He influenced my painting and delighted me." Close to members of the Provincetown Players group, she became an activist in the Art Association and a leader in the social life of the colony. She produced moody landscapes where small figures sometimes brace themselves against the wind under somber or turbulent skies. "When I paint a landscape," she said, "it is never a literal representation, but what I feel about what I see." She often paints outdoors and once painted Highland Light with a booming gale tossing her gear. In Hawthorne's class she met *Jerry Farnsworth* (1895–   ), a southern-born New Yorker. In 1925 they were married and bought an old house in North Truro where they set up separate studios. Farnsworth made a national reputation as a portrait painter (he painted President Truman and also his mother). Recently he has become best-known for studies of children. In 1943 they opened a school in North Truro where Farnsworth trained students according to the Hawthorne method of painting with the knife.

Charles A. Kaeselau (1889–1970) came to Provincetown in the early 1920's with a group from the Chicago Art Institute that included Vaclav Vytlacil (1890–   ), Karl Knaths, Cameron Booth and Ross Moffett. He followed John Noble as director of the Art Association (1923) and was active in the community until his death in 1972. To judge by his work in the collection of the town, his landscapes of the harbor front were appealingly atmospheric, quiet in color and mood.

Of the Precisionists who came to Provincetown, hoping to interpret American landscape via Cubist-Realism, *Niles Spencer* (1893–1952) stayed nearly as long as Demuth (15 years) after his arrival in the mid-1930's. A thoughtful and reserved man with no trace of the bohemian, he was a friend of the novelist, John Dos Passos. Although he knew Demuth and may have been somewhat influenced by his machine-age subjects, in his own work in this genre there was no hint of irony.

From the amiable chaos of Provincetown's lanes and tumbling rooftops — seemingly unpromising for an artist in search of a sense of stability and order —

Provincetown skyline from the wharf. From left to right: Universalist Church, Town Hall and Pilgrim Monument — Photograph courtesy of Cyril Patrick

Niles Spencer managed to extract trim, unpeopled, geometric structures true to the essentials of the scene. In early works like *Down the Hill,* 1924, and *New England Landscape* (collection of Albright Knox Gallery, Buffalo), open lots, backs of houses, and a church, he used angular perspectives and painterly passages that he would eliminate in his later style.

In the late 1920's, when he was working in the south of France with Monroe Wheeler and Glenway Westcott, Spencer learned that the Provincetown studio in which he had worked was for sale, and immediately made arrangements to buy it with funds from his successful second one-man show at the Daniel Gallery in New York. In 1937 he executed, entirely in Provincetown, a twenty-foot mural commissioned by the U.S. Treasury Department for the Post Office of the town of Aliquippa, Pennsylvania, representing its river-front steel mills and industrial complex. After completing this in his spare, geometrically simplified manner, Spencer was increasingly drawn to industrial subjects. After the summer of 1940 he did not return to Provincetown. He died in 1952 at Dingman's Ferry, Pennsylvania.

The watercolors of *John Whorf* (1903–1959) — and watercolor was his exclusive medium after 1932 — including scores of Cape End marine subjects, were collected by Rosalind Russell, Vincent Price, the Pitti Gallery in Florence, and even by John Singer Sargent. Whorf studied with Hawthorne in the mid-twenties, then returned to Provincetown every summer for the rest of his life, living there year-round at some periods not far from the Shore Galleries that handled his work there and in Boston. In 1940 he occupied the famous Waugh house, later the oldest house in Provincetown at 72 Commercial. Perhaps his best known residence was on West Vine Street.

From a colorful family — his father was a well-known commercial illustrator, his brother, Richard Whorf, a popular Hollywood actor — the artist was regarded as a "character." He walked with a cane, the result of a bout with polio when he was 17, and wore a jaunty yachtman's cap. At the Beachcombers' he favored salty language; some of his best epithets were reserved for the despised abstractionists. He once joined Richard Miller in a stunt in which they managed to get past the "modern" jury of the Art Association a canvas they had daubed with crazy abandon, then titled "Hence the Pyramids," and signed "Ad Wolgast," the name of an old-time prize fighter.

The outdoor subjects of his own conservative paintings were sketched on the spot, then painted in the studio with an attractive bravura that owed much to his special instruction from Sargent. His vigorously extroverted reports on the life of sea and shore in all seasons brought him a wide reputation and financial success. He remained an influential figure until his death.

If the reputation of Hawthorne drew three young students from the John Heron Institute in Indianapolis to Provincetown, it was the sea-girt landscape that kept them at the Cape End year-round for the rest of their days. They were *Philip Malicoat* (1908–   ), *Bruce McKain* (1900–   ) and (to wind up in Truro) George Yater (1910–   ). Philip Malicoat came in 1929, studied two years with Hawthorne and, after the teacher's death, worked another two years under his assistant, Henry Hensche (1901–   ). But his most important experience was in the extensive drawing he did at that time with Edwin Dickinson. Malicoat's work reflects less the precision of Dickinson than a broad, painterly response to a landscape nuanced in greys. Malicoat adds deep, murky blues and sparse accents of off-whites and blacks. His simplifications underline a quality of vastness and mystery in nature.

The whitening "patriarchal" beard that adds an enigmatic note in his strikingly composed self-portraits is deceptive since he is still young enough to lead a strenuous outdoor life. During World War II he fished for two years with

53

Provincetown Art Association — 1961. Left to right: Umberto Romano, Seong
Moy, George Yater, Henry Hensche, Byron Browne, Morris Davidson, Ross
Moffett, Irving Marantz, Henry Botkin, Joe Kaplan, Peter Busa, Bruce McKain,
Lily Harmon, Gerrit Hondius, Harry Engel, Ben Wolf.
Photograph by Arnold Newman

Manny Zora, "the sea fox," and shipped out again during extended studies at the Oceanographic Institute at Woods Hole.

Besides the studio behind his home at 320 Bradford Street, where he now lives, he also paints at a picturesque elevated studio built of weathered boards on an isolated stretch of dunes overlooking his favorite subject: the wild Atlantic shore. At the Group Gallery he has shown not only his paintings of the Cape but also scenes painted on trips to Greece, Italy and France. He has been active on the advisory staff of the Fine Arts Work Center and was recently given a one man show of his paintings at the Hudson Walker Gallery on Pearl Street.

Bruce McKain hitchhiked to Provincetown in 1928, studied with Hawthorne for two years, and spent his first winter there in 1932–33. Except for a stint of war work in Stonington, Connecticut, he has lived there ever since in a pleasant house just off Commercial Street with a studio on the second floor. Dedicated to on-the-spot painting, he manages to work on his harbor scenes from various waterfront buildings. He would not improvise a cloud that the particular weather and time of day did not provide. A good bit of the direct, objectively-visual approach of Hawthorne's teaching is still to be seen in McKain's broad, confident handling of the brush and restrained, atmospheric color.

For a fifteen-year period after Bruce McKain relinquished the post in 1947, *George Yater,* his schoolmate from Indianapolis, was director of the Provincetown Art Association. He remained active even after he moved to a spacious house in a wooded section of Truro. Yater came to Provincetown in 1931, too late to study with Hawthorne; for four years he studied with Henry Hensche, Hawthorne's former assistant. With his light-toned palette and vibrant brush, Yater seems the most Impressionist of the three from Indianapolis, especially in his large oils. In his teaching, Hawthorne urged students to try to discover beauty in things that were plain or even ugly. Although this dictum must have come to Yater second hand, he has sometimes succeeded admirably in doing just that. One example is his earlier watercolor of the old Provincetown ice plant. In a recent watercolor he created an arresting image from a row of identical bungalows monotonously strung out along the approach to Provincetown.

When *Maurice Sterne* (1878–1957) first came to Provincetown in 1915, he had just returned from a decade abroad climaxed by an extended stay on the Island of Bali. A tide of popularity greeted his gently geometricized paintings of natives and tropical settings — they were Cezannesque without destroying the exotic appeal of the subject. This restrained stylized modernism was, however, far from the precise realism he had been taught by Thomas Eakins at the New York Academy. Artistic daring, added to the foreign good looks of the Russian-born artist, made him a "culture hero" of the moment to some intellectuals. He was married to Mabel Dodge on the Cape in the summer of 1917 and painted from a famous spot in the dunes during a rather hectic summer. Two years later they were divorced.

Decades later, no longer quite so famous but still covered with international honors from his sculpture as well as painting, Sterne returned to Provincetown with his second wife, ballet dancer Vera Segal, and bought a substantial house in the East End. He worked there summers — painting and teaching privately — almost until his death in 1957. He was honored by a memorial exhibition of his work at the Art Association.

Among the artists who showed at the Art Association between 1927 and 1932 in the separate modern exhibitions was (Harry) *Lee Gatch* (1902–1968), known in later years for the lyrical semi-abstract paintings he produced from his studio-house deep in the woods of Lambertville, Pennsylvania. A close friend of Karl Knaths, he shared a need to live close to nature and to create around the nature experience a mystical, personal philosophy. After achieving an early competence as a Cubist, he turned away from rigorous angular flatness. By the

The Back Shore — Photograph courtesy of Cyril Patrick

time he was staying and exhibiting in Provincetown, he had developed a style of ovals combined with wedge-shapes in soft, off-focus tones that encompassed limited references to distance. Linear elements offered clues to the symbolic meanings of his Pantheistic credo.

Also exhibiting at that time was *Elsie Driggs* (1898–   ), who acquired an early fame as a Precisionist from her widely exhibited painting of the Bethlehem Steel complex. Since her interests were diverse and her style often more fluid, she rejected the "Precisionist" label. In Provincetown, like Gatch, she found motifs in the landscape. Subsequently they were married.

From his cozy house in the East End on the Bay, where he spent summers from the 1950's, *Sol Wilson* (1897–1970) turned out paintings of the shore and other settings, spontaneously sketched on his trips up-Cape, in which small figures usually played a part, but seldom as active protagonists. Gathered in groups near the water, often at dusk or near nightfall, they seem to be witnessing a view that is somewhat mysterious but never awesome. His brush, loaded with off-blacks, plied loosely but knowingly through close tones, created an intimate world instantly recognizable as his own. The Art Association held a memorial exhibition of his work after he died in 1975.

Truro

If *Ben Shahn*'s daughter, Judith Shahn, is correct in guessing that the years her father spent summers in a house in Truro were in the very late 1920's and/or early 1930's, it was a period of critical change in his work. The Russian-born artist who had come to the U.S. with his family when he was twelve, had returned to Europe for travel and study in 1925 and again in 1927. Subsequently he worked in a style influenced by George Rouault. Between 1931 and 1934 he was at work, in a contrastingly and precisely graphic manner, on his now famous series of small paintings based on the lives of Sacco and Vanzetti, whose executions in 1927 had aroused protests around the world. (Shahn's mural on this theme, "The Passion of Sacco and Vanzetti," of 1967, graces the exterior of Huntington B. Crouse Hall on the Syracuse University campus.) Along with his parallel Tom Mooney series, these works launched his new career as a spokesman for political and social causes.

It may be that the summers in Truro afforded a needed change from the tight technique of gouache to the spontaneity of sketching his infant daughter, Judith, and from programatic themes to the direct visual response to bathers gathered on the beach with their bright-colored hats and umbrellas. Judith Shahn writes: "I was amused to see that one of the reproductions in the Kennedy Gallery catalog for Ben's show in 1969 was titled 'Nude Bathers Truro.' With all the current uproar about nude bathing here, I thought it was of some interest." In oils Shahn painted a portrait of photographer Walker Evans with whom he held a joint show around 1930 in a neighbor's barn.

A simplified Expressionism was basic to the painting of a number of artists working in the Truro area, among them *Morris Kantor* (1896–1974), who lived with his wife, Martha, not far from the Hoppers. When Kantor abandoned Cubist abstraction around 1924, there was nothing half-hearted in his return to nature. In fact he painted not only from on-the-spot observation but completely out-of-doors, such apparently difficult subjects as *Dunes at Sunset, Shipwreck on the Shore, South Truro Church* and *Storm Over the Bay,* all in the late 1930's. Kantor was among the new exhibitors in the modern shows at the Provincetown Art Association during the period from 1933 to 1936.

Henry Varnum Poor (1888–1970), commuting summers to Maine where he held a teaching post, was also devoted to his home in Truro, and found time to sketch in pastels and paint in watercolor the Pamet Inlet meadow and nearby

Hans Hofmann and Maria, 1960. Hofmann photograph by Arnold Newman

hills. Poor was asked as a modern, along with Morris Kantor and Niles Spencer, to the first partly-invitational exhibition inaugurated in 1939. George Biddle was invited as a modern alternate.

The years immediately following the end of World War II signaled for many Cape artists a deeply-longed-for return to a personal and intimate expression after years of WPA projects, murals and war work — all public and impersonal. One of the most distinguished arrivals of that time was *George Biddle* (1885–1973), son of an illustrious Philadelphia family, whose more illustrational work was known to millions through his paintings of war locales when he was Chairman of the War Department Art Committee. In 1946, shortly after his marriage to sculptor Helene Sardeau (1899–1968), they bought a Revolutionary-period house in Truro with provision for separate studios. For the more relaxed style in which he painted his surroundings on the Cape, Biddle gave credit to the influence of Japanese prints, Edgar Degas and his old friend, Mary Cassatt. In many years abroad he had counted among his friends James Joyce, Gertrude Stein and Jules Pascin. He had once been engaged to opera star Grace Moore for two years and had lived for a month with Mexican muralist Diego Rivera. Biddle's murals are in Washington, D.C., in Rio de Janeiro, Brazil, and Mexico City.

An artist who rose to more than regional prominence in the 1930's was *Charles Heinz* (1885–1953). He showed with the traditional group in the period between 1928 and 1932 and during the following several years served on traditional juries. But by 1937 the juicy paint quality and glowing color of his Provincetown scenes looked quite modern to some critics. The *New York Times'* critic, Edward Alden Jewel, reproduced a painting by Heinz and complained he could no longer tell the traditionalist from the moderns. Two years later William Germain Dooley, critic of the *Boston Transcript,* wrote: "Charles Heinz . . . emerges as a forceful painter and an original colorist . . . He has matured a style, given it sensuous throbbing light and color, a clarity of bold forms. His work is coming into the top rank of New England art." His painting of back yards in the collection of the Provincetown Art Association is a fine example of his color and painterly touch. He was a trustee of the Art Association between 1948 and 1950.

Hans Hofmann and the Abstract Expressionists

When *Hans Hofmann* came to America in 1930 it was in response to an invitation to teach at the University of California at Berkeley in the summer. His plan was, after establishing himself as a teacher, to take groups of students back to Europe, probably to Capri, for summer extension classes in the same way that he had customarily conducted students from his Munich school. Initially sojourning in Bavarian mountain villages, they had later summered at Ragusa, at Mediterranean St. Tropez as well as Capri. But during Hofmann's first years in the United States, Hitler was consolidating his Nazi regime; Hofmann was warned that if he persisted in his project for summers abroad it would be all but impossible for him to return. It is likely that the Provincetown summer school came into being as an eventual substitute — a summer by the sea with himself in charge of a student flock, but transposed to this side of the Atlantic.

Some of his closest students in Provincetown believe that Hofmann would have gravitated to America even if his Munich school had not been hounded by a repressive regime. Fritz Bultman said: "He was by temperament and outlook astonishingly American; he adored Roosevelt, was deeply moved by his death." He was buoyantly optimistic, physically vigorous, endlessly energetic and devoted to work. Having been an inventor in his youth, he had a respect for

Hans Hofmann in his studio, Christmas Eve, 1965. From left to right, John Snow, Bernie Beckman, Karl Knaths and Hans Hofmann.

technology. His art theories about the "push and pull" of spatial relationships on the canvas were just as real and demonstrable to him as the laws of mechanics.

Before emigrating Hofmann had confirmed that in spite of his never surmounted difficulties with the English language, he was able to communicate and convey his aesthetic doctrine to the Americans who found their way to his Munich school in the 1920's. Among them were Louise Nevelson, Vaclav Vytlacil, Cameron Booth, Ludwig Sander.

From their reports word filtered back to American schools and universities that Hofmann was an inspired teacher, that his understanding of modern art was unique, his method revolutionary. He had more than enough invitations to teach. In 1932 and 1933 he taught winters at the Art Students League in New York, summers at the Thurn School in Gloucester, Massachusetts. In 1933 he founded the Hans Hofmann School of Fine Arts on Ninth Street (later moved to Eighth Street) in Greenwich Village. The following summer he opened his summer school in Provincetown.

Hawthorne died in 1930. Years later Hofmann was to maintain that it was his destiny to fill the vacuum. Actually it was not until after World War II that his school could be compared in enrollment and influence to Hawthorne's. In the meantime his school occupied the building on Miller Hill that had housed the Hawthorne classes. Provincetown was not inclined to accept as a replacement for their venerated "father figure," a foreigner with incomprehensible English whose ideas on art conformed neither to the doctrines of the traditionalists nor to those of the accepted moderns. An early and devoted Hofmann student, William Freed, remembers that in the 1930's the school was held in such low regard that he did not openly admit he was attending it.

In his early fifties, Hofmann was well-built (later he was to become more robust) with a healthy fair complexion, lively blue eyes and shock of light brown hair streaked with grey. He was an intrepid swimmer, a tireless walker; his *joie de vivre* was evident in his love of good food and good wines. He was not a businessman and the school was often in the red. His sympathy with the students led him to extend scholarships lavishly; sometimes half those enrolled were not paying. It was not until Mrs. Hofmann (Miz) arrived in August 1939 with her astute business sense, that the school was put on a better footing financially.

The great post-war expansion of the school followed a trying and near disastrous time when classes functioned peripatetically. The Hofmanns were shocked when the Hawthorne property they had rented for a decade was suddenly sold in 1944, without warning, to Morris Davidson who subsequently conducted his school there. Hofmann's classes met in any vacant space. Often it was in the unusual studio building near Miller Hill that Fritz Bultman was erecting with the architectural collaboration of Tony Smith; it was literally built around the classes at work on the site.

Then by what seemed a miracle, the great Waugh studio, along with his colonial house, was available on Commercial Street at Nickerson, on the West End, into which they moved in 1946. The high-vaulted studio with its great beams and picturesque balcony was splended for students, ideal for Hofmann's now thronged critique sessions. The element of theater in the place brought out Hofmann's latent gifts as an evangelist for modern art and for the life of art. His talks attained a new level of dramatic intensity.

The old house itself was transformed by the imaginative innovations of Miz Hofmann who had been an artist in her own right. Her garden of hollyhocks, larkspur and other colorful blooms flourished along the entrance and more strikingly as a setting for the tiled patio on the side. An even more dramatic transformation of color took place in the upstairs rooms where floors and ceilings were painted in different, solidly brilliant hues, and the furniture such as bureaus and chests painted in a color of maximum — often complementary — contrasts:

Forum 49 — Courtesy of Mrs. Adolph Gottlieb.
Left to right: Blanche Lazzell, Morris Davidson, unidentified, Perle Fine, unidentified, Adolph Gottlieb, Karl Knaths, Weldon Kees, unidentified, Dante, Lawrence Kupferman, unidentified, unidentified, unidentified, Kenneth Campbell, Judith Rothschild, Boris Margo, unidentified, Leo Manso, Peter Busa, Fritz Bultman, John Grillo, William Freed.
Photograph by Bill Witt

violet furniture against yellow floor, or green against red-orange. With the foil of the white walls, the effect of the boldly massed colors was Matisse-like; surprisingly the paintings by Hofmann and other masters were not diminished by this setting.

In the mornings students drew from the model or from still-life with charcoal or crayon; they were asked to focus not on likeness or representation, but on the way the forms activated the surrounding space. In his criticisms — and he tried to get to each student — Hofmann did not so much explain as demonstrate where tensions were manifested and how the space was pushing here or pulling there. To the dismay of new students (and the outrage of some educators) he sometimes tore a work in progress right down the middle to show how a slight discrepancy between the halves revealed tensions.

Students painted on their own outside the classroom and brought the finished canvases to the Friday criticism. Here Hofmann's remarks on each canvas were addressed to an audience that usually included a number of visitors along with the class. In his interpretation of the Cubist aesthetic, a true perception of space was different for each individual according to his temperament. Discovering space was discovering the self. The concept of "forming with color" was often illustrated with examples from Matisse and his decorative paintings that were "beyond decoration." By showing examples of special composition from old masters (Delacroix, Titian, Rembrandt) as well as moderns, Hofmann opened up the whole history of art to a new perception.

It was inspiring and it was confusing. Many who entered his classes expecting to be taught how to make an abstract painting, quickly dropped out when they discovered he offered no ready formulas. For others months passed before they had an inkling of what he was talking about. Wolf Kahn said that even advanced students suffered from chronic cultural indigestion. At every stage of their work they were challenged by a multiplicity of choices, and Hofmann was not primarily interested in having the student produce a finished picture. More important was the student's experience of the full range of creative possibility. After weeks of painting on a single canvas that had been constantly reworked in the light of progressively-embraced concepts, each stage had cancelled out the previous one. Wolf Kahn said, "A canvas might come to have the worked-over look of a DeKooning; one of my charcoal drawings in the end most often resembled a grey rag." When students did get to see some of Hofmann's paintings (he concealed them from pupils as long as possible), often they were unimpressed; they also dismissed as "mere decoration" much of the work of other artists, soon to be called "abstract-expressionists."

Confronted with his polyglot speech, students supplied their own versions of what they guessed he had said. When this was reported back to him he was baffled; he said: "It was never right!" Partially deaf since youth (he wore a hearing aid), he had never heard English clearly, as Fritz Bultman has observed. He accented syllables according to some odd and arbitrary system of his own (talented was always "tal-EN-ted") and inserted words into sentences structured in the German way; sometimes he finished them out with French phrases.

For those who stayed with him, the impact of Hofmann's teaching was enormous. Painter and sculptor Louise Pershing, who came from Pittsburgh for several summers, said: "When you studied with Hofmann your whole life changed: not only your work but the way you dressed, dined, the books you read, your friends and recreations changed. Your idea of what life was about changed."

"The canvas was a unity on which every 'millimeter' was to be charged with life, and function and the shifting of a millimeter changed the inner relationship of the whole creation," recalled Fritz Bultman in a lecture on Hofmann at the Smithsonian Institution. "Everything affected the whole and nothing less than the whole was to be the goal of the artist-student's experience."

Yet it was in Provincetown that Hofmann was confronted with apparent defections from his teachings. He told me, "Some of my best students were those who turned against me."

Forum '49

A milestone summer in Provincetown was 1949. An expansive Hans Hofmann was entering a fertile period in his work, and his school was at the height of its influence (artists of all persuasions now crowded into his weekly criticisms — early abstractionist Blanche Lazzell was a regular). Many New York vanguard painters were in and out of town along with a California contingent and, of course, the resident Abstract Expressionsists. The new art currents that had seemed diffused only a season or so before were now being defined and elaborated not only to other artists but also to a newly arrived throng of admiring bystanders in animated gatherings in studios, cafes and on beaches. For the first time painters were talking to writers and poets on an equal footing; they shared an upsurge of excitement and expectation and a sense that they were living through a time of significant cultural change.

If art history was indeed in the making, the emerging questions, ideas and concepts could not be allowed to evaporate — they needed to be aired in an organized and on-going exchange. The idea of Forum '49, a summer-long series of programs, was probably the brain-child of poet and painter *Weldon Kees* (1914–1955); he had enthusiastic co-founders in artist Fritz Bultman (1919–   ), and writer-and-poet Cecil Hemley, then living year-round in Provincetown. Hemley recruited his cousin, Adolph Gottlieb. From the beginning Hans Hofmann and Karl Knaths were actively involved. Bultman recalls that Kees was the "prime mover and shaker," he had the dedication, the contacts and he also had a car, an old one he had bought from Mark Rothko who called it Tiresias. Weldon Kees was probably best known as an authority on jazz who also played jazz-piano. Though he was just in his thirties and looked even younger, he had hobnobbed with the jazz greats in New Orleans. A poet with two published books of verse to his credit (*The Last Man* and *The Fall of the Magicians*), Kees had won the Blumenthal Prize for poetry in 1948. He was a frequent contributor to the *New Yorker.* If his poems were often bitter and tragic, his paintings and collages (in a one man show at the Peridot Gallery in November 1948) were notable for joyous, singing color.

The problem of a space for the forums was solved when it turned out that a large place that had formerly been the Ford Garage at 200 Commercial Street could be shared with a new art gallery just being inaugurated by Don Witherstine as an extension to his successful Shore Studios Gallery in the West End (probably the earliest commerical gallery in Provincetown). The name, Gallery 200, for the new space was applied during that summer to both Forum '49 and the gallery operation. Whitewashed by a brigade led by Miz Hofmann and furnished with seating for 200, Forum '49 was ready to open on July 3rd. Even with these spacious quarters it was necessary to turn away 500 person on the opening night.

The first subject, "What is an Artist?" was debated by four Cape panelists: Hans Hofmann, George Biddle, Adolph Gottlieb and Serge Chermayeff. A representational painter and author of international reputation, Biddle emphasized the importance of "an attitude toward life in painting," whether the idiom be realistic or abstract. After Chermayeff was introduced by Weldon Kees as head of the Chicago Institute of Design, a painter, writer and lecturer, he said, "The artist was only another specialist in a world of specialists." The artist is a craftsman like a plumber. "The tool or message that works has always been accepted." Adolph Gottlieb attacked the "good craftsmanship" view. He said,

"The artist must take the risk of creating works that will not be recognized as art," and referred to "the bad picture, well done, that flatters the taste of the general public." Hans Hofmann, as the final speaker, admitted that he did not know what an artist is — but he did know what makes an artist. "Only the man equipped with creative instincts and a searching mind is destined to become an artist. Talent is everywhere but it doesn't make an artist. It's often a handicap, it invites cleverness."

A highlight of the accompanying exhibit of 50 artists was the room devoted to the work of four Provincetown pioneers in abstract art: Oliver Chaffee was represented by an abstraction derived from foliage patterns, E. Ambrose Webster by a cubist work and two decorative flower subjects. Works by both the late Agnes Weinrich and Blanche Lazzell (the only survivor), with their subdued colors and cutout shapes, were rated "most contemporary" by Elaine de Kooning. Also winning critical approval were two freshly-painted canvases by Hofmann, the diagonally-patterned *Spots and Stripes* by Knaths, *Eight-armed Dancer* by Byron Browne, *Expectations of Evil* by Gottlieb, and Motherwell's small *At Five in the Afternoon*. Jackson Pollock was represented by two intricately spattered multi-colored paintings called "the most striking" by Elaine de Kooning.

The regular Thursday evening programs got under way on July 7 with Dwight Macdonald, summering in Wellfleet, speaking on "The Dream World of Soviet Bureaucracy." His talk was advertised as "a searing exposé of the men who rule Russia and Russia's ruthless totalitarianism." This was followed July 14 by "American Jazz Music: the 1920's" with records by Jelly-Roll Morton, Louis Armstrong, Johnny Dodds, Kid Cry, Bessie Smith and a commentary by Weldon Kees who said: "Authentic Jazz music — a completely American phenomenon is today almost a buried music in its own country ... we've been all but sunk by crooners, swing bands, and devotees of the bebop school." He urged Americans to catch up with Europe's early appreciation of New Orleans and Dixieland music. The program on July 21 was devoted to a showing of rare early films from the collection of Joseph Cornell, including the magical trick movies of French pioneer, Melies. A second feature was "104th Street: Notes for a Documentary" by Helen Levitt and Janice Loeb from Wellfleet.

By the end of July there was no doubt that the first month of Forum '49 had been a success. With an admission fee of sixty cents, attendance had broken records even on hot and sultry nights. The admission charge barely covered basic expenses, but then these were kept to a minimum. Even the most celebrated speakers were paid only with a bottle of Scotch, but they were put up for the night by the artists and by their close friends. An added attraction was that the forums were always followed by lively parties, usually at Weathering Heights, with Weldon Kees playing jazz piano and uninhibited dancing until all hours.

The exhibition had been called "a show New York or Paris might be proud to have" and was credited with revealing "the roots of visual abstract work that had its beginnings in Provincetown not long after World War I." Clement Greenberg had called the programs "the most lively thing of its sort ever presented in the summer — and perhaps in the winter too." The forums planned for August were even more provocative.

Recordings of James Joyce and T. S. Eliot reading from their own works were featured on the first Thursday evening, followed by a commentary from Nathan (Nat) Halper on Joyce's *Finnegan's Wake*. (Halper, a Joyce scholar and a long time Provincetown resident, was a contributor to *The New Republic, Partisan Review* and *Commentary*.) Poet and critic, Howard Nemerov discussed the poetry of Eliot.

The August 11th forum with the topic "French Art vs. U.S. Art Today" was by far the most controversial of the series for the artists themselves; its clashes are still vividly remembered today. It revealed a divergence of attitudes that had been developing since the wartime years. In 1944 Jackson Pollock had said (in an interview in the February 1944 issue of *Arts and Architecture*): "The idea of an isolated American painting, so popular in this country during the thirties, seems absurd to me, just as the idea of creating a purely American mathematics or physics would seem absurd ... the basic problems of contemporary painting are independent of any country ... the two artists that I admire most, Picasso and Miro, are still abroad." One year earlier, in 1943, Adolph Gottlieb and Mark Rothko in their famous letter to the *New York Times* had ignored ties to Europe and emphasized a kinship with primitive art. Others in the interim had lauded the rough vitality of American art as contrasted with the tasteful subtleties of "the French cuisine." After the war when Americans had a chance to see, usually in reproduction, the work of the French painters of the post-Picasso generation, many were scornful of ingratiating or decorative qualities. Adolph Gottlieb was moderator and also a speaker at this often unruly session of Forum '49; he led off with a query as to whether the pride which the French always have taken in their art has provided a healthy climate for French artists. The *New York Times* critic, Stuart Preston, contended that an artist must be rooted in the soil of his land, and said that the collapse of a vital sustaining tradition has been "more disastrous for French art than it would be for America. The American artist is accustomed to being an isloated practitioner, the French artist tends to swim in schools, the larger the better." Karl Knaths disagreed: "There is a region of the mind as well as the soil." He though the plastic sensibility of the artist the "decisive factor in the modern art movement." Paris had taken the lead because the artists of other countries "lacked the tradition of the French." Paul Mocsanyi, art critic for the United Press, countered with the thought that it may be just the isolation of the American artist with consequent introspection and subjectivity, that leads to a great school of American art. Frederick Wight, educational director of the Boston Museum of Contemporary Art, agreed with those who saw a "falling off" of French art. Robert Motherwell, stressing the intense subjectivity of the modern artist, said: "There is a difficulty of communication because a community or a culture no longer exists."

There is no record that Hans Hofmann took part in the discussion — his deafness was often a barrier — but he was deeply offended by what he took to be a denigration of the art of Paris (the source of the art concepts that guided his teaching). Following the forum a one-page protest headed "Ostrich Attitudes in the Arts" was circulated. Signed by Hofmann and Bultman it read (in part): "The estate of the arts should never be narrowed to a national basis — particularly by the artist. Paris's [sic] humanism has given the opportunity of free development of such artists as the Spaniards — Picasso, Gris, Miro; the Swiss — Klee, Corbusier, Giacometti; the Russians — Kandinsky, Chagall; the Rumanian — Brancusi; the Irishman — Joyce; the Americans — Stein, Man Ray, Carles; the Pole — Lipchitz and many others.... We earnestly hope that artistic creation in America will develop the same fruitful ground to equal such an example."

The remaining August forums were lively but less divisive. "Direction of 20th-Century Architecture" was discussed by two authorities both born in Hungary and both with summer homes in Wellfleet. Gyorgy Kepes (1906–   ), painter, photographer, designer, author of the *Language of Vision* (then in its sixth printing), and head of the Center for Advanced Visual Studies at Massachusetts Institute of Technology, was expected to challenge the Bauhaus point of view of Marcel Breuer (1902–   ), who had been a teacher at the Bauhaus, founded by Walter Gropius in 1919. Best-known as the developer of tubular furniture, Breuer had recently designed a controversial one-family house for New York's Museum of Modern Art.

Donald Slesinger was chairman of the August 25 forum on "Finding Yourself Through Psychoanalysis," with a galaxy of experts including Gerardus Beekman, Dr. Wilfred Bloomberg, Dr. Leo Spiegel and the very well-known Dr. Clara

Thompson. The season wound up on September first with "Everybody's Forum." Memorable and interesting now in the light of the women's movement, were Elaine de Kooning's appreciative reflections on the art of Mary Cassatt.

Forum '49 marked a gradual change from the immediate postwar period when very little public attention was paid to artists' gatherings, their talks or their works. If change was inevitable — national and even international changes in the art world were operative — at least this introduction to a new sophistication had been kept on an impressively high level due to the broad horizons of those who organized it. A somber footnote comes from Fritz Bultman; speaking of the Forum's prime mover, Weldon Kees: "He was the most gifted and lively person of that whole epoch … (an individual of) complete culture and terribly witty. He disappeared, his car found near or on the Golden Gate Bridge. His body was never found.

Hans Hofmann: His Work

With verve and spontaneity Hofmann had drawn the Cape landscape in the 1950's and 1940's — sometimes with matchsticks dipped in ink — and he had painted the waterfront in planes ablaze with oranges, yellows and blues. His wintertime still-lifes were more reworked to clarify cubist structure. Partly in response to the automatism developed by the Abstract Expressionists in the later forties, Hofmann was moving away from Cubist structures into a more open space where the brush, running with washes or loaded with paint, was charged with a racing momentum. In the idea of "empathy" Hoffman found a bridge between his customary reliance on nature as a source and the intensification of inherent qualities in the paint and materials. Miro, an artist he admired — the Miro canvas he owned was a prime treasure — was an example of an artist oriented to nature who made eloquent use of automatic elements.

A 1949 exhibition of his work in Paris was a milestone in his effort to recover his place in the world as an artist. But it was not until after he gave up teaching in 1958 (he was then 78) that he won full recognition for his painting. Fritz Bultman noted a new richness and serenity in the lives of the Hofmanns at this period. He said: "One felt in both of them, a great refining of means and a closeness at this period of their lives. They would drive to see the sunsets that on the Cape in the autumn are unusually beautiful and reflect the landscape's richness. It is this quality that one senses in his abstract paintings at this late time. It was on one of these rides that Hans expressed his deep desire 'to paint out of doors again from nature' with all he knew now."

Notable in the 1960's was growth in two directions, one marked by sweeping organic rhythms, the other by thickly impastoed planes of color composed in a generally rectilinear structure (sometimes in juxtaposition with loosely brushed areas). In the latter which Hofmann called his "quantum paintings," he came closest to realizing his ideal of forming with color and, without imposing a structure, forcing the eye to comprehend one, perhaps by making jumps comparable to those ascribed to the atom in quantum theory.

The full-scale exhibition of his work at the Museum of Modern Art in 1963 coincided with the death of Mrs. Hofmann following surgery. Working in what he called "a negative ecstasy," Hofmann intensified his work. He had always dreamed of matching Titian's nine decades of creativity but fell short of realizing it by four years — he was eighty-six years old when he died of a heart attack in 1966.

The Hofmann Milieu: Abstract Painters

A second circle coexisting with the relatively older Abstract Expressionists, was composed of students of Hans Hofmann: one-time pupils now friends of the teacher's and staying on in Provincetown as residents and another younger group of those just completing classes (many funded for a season by the G.I. Bill) who had no lasting commitment to the colony. In 1947 the latter included a galaxy of talent; their works were exhibited at the Seligmann Gallery in New York, a selection made by Hofmann and Clement Greenberg, and called *New Provincetown 1947.* Represented, among others, were Paul Georges, Wolf Kahn, Robert Goodnough, Paul Resika, Seymour Reminick and Leatrice Rose. Bob DeNiro also joined the Hofmann class at about this time, supporting himself through rough and exhausting work at the ice house. Many of this class did not return except one decade later for the funeral of Jan Müller. Paul Resika remembers that he idolized Hofmann but at that time, 1947, he had not yet had a chance to explore traditional classical modes of painting, he was not ready to think about painting in rigorously abstract terms. Some of the others who were as much in rebellion against Hofmann's method as they were devoted to him, were in a similar plight. Since 1964 Resika has been engaged in realistic painting of woodsy areas near his studio in Wellfleet. "Now my feeling about Hofmann's teaching is the complete reverse," he said. "He was right. Today I believe more and more in what he said."

A different, less conflicted outlook was shared by most of the earlier students who had stayed on in the town. They were neither so plagued by a longing for traditional representation as some of the younger students, nor were they so single-mindedly bent on the pursuit of the ultimate and universal in art as the older Abstract Expressionists. They did not necessarily share the Abstract Expressionists' abhorence of any trace of the provincial, they were more apt to be interested in artists of local reputation. Hofmann himself, having proved his cosmopolitanism through a decade in Paris, felt no such obstacles to the appreciation of those who had less than international fame; he fell completely under the spell of Ryder when he first came to the United States, and he admired Hawthorne as a painter and a powerful temperament. Hofmann's emphasis on the resources to be found in exterior nature (the model, still life, landscape) as well as interior nature (the unconscious) left many paths open to the artist.

In recalling his lifetime association and friendship with Hofmann in his talk at the Smithsonian (November 1976), Fritz Bultman said: "It should be pointed out that his concept of the picture was as part of the greater experience of nature. This was not nature as a scene or a motif but as a process of living parts, including also the artist and the canvas." A breadth of concept has enabled Bultman to function simultaneously as a painter, sculptor, collagist and, working from the model, to produce large scale drawings with a classical purity of line.

Having grown up in a family well-established in New Orleans, *Fritz Bultman* (born in 1919) had taken off for Germany when he was sixteen but was thwarted by the repressions of the Hitler regime from his hope of studying at the Bauhaus. In Munich he shared the teacher's apartment with Mrs. Hofmann and she became a surrogate mother. After his return to the U.S., he entered Hofmann's classes and, both in Provincetown and in New York during the winters, lived close to "Miz" Hofmann and was also in constant touch with Hans. His studies continued in Provincetown from 1939 to 1942. Then, following his marriage to Jeanne Lawson, he built a hilltop frame house in a wooded section in the East End and lived there with his family during most of the war years. The proximity of studios and ample gardens below is not by accident since many of his themes derive from working in the garden. One such idea (not a motif but a system of relationships) was later reflected in paintings, a sculpture and in the shapes that emerged in a collage. Bultman said: "I love the robustness of nature. Nature is as important to me as to Hofmann but I use it differently."

Myron Stout (1908–   ) who has lived year round in Provincetown for decades, grew up in Denton, Texas. Preparing for a career in teaching, he obtained his BA and Masters degrees at Teachers College, Columbia. It was not until he was established in a teaching post in Hawaii that his interest focused seriously on painting, and he longed to be in New York where Americans were breaking new ground in the arts. After he heard through fellow Texan, Toni La Selle, of the Hofmann summer school, he crossed the Pacific and the Continent each summer from 1947 to 1952. Stout said: "I began to connect with myself as I never had before." In those years he was at the center of a circle of young pace-setters.

After phases in which he pursued "a dynamic play of elements" first in a classical then in a more baroque space, he began in the fifties to work entirely with black and white. While many of his colleagues were obsessed with the quick, gestural attack with paint, he took an opposite attack: a slow, deliberate approach in which the "millimeter's difference" so often emphasized by Hofmann, could be crucial. Work might extend into years while a contour is adjusted an eighth inch or a curve showed to an infinitesimal degree. The process of adjustment is as mysterious as the relationship of shapes is ambiguous: white and black, positive and negative, seeming to exchange places. He can never produce enough to satisfy the demand of collectors.

His studio-apartment at 4 Brewster Street is usually piled high with books on a wide range of subjects. His interests are catholic, his friends and acquaintances legion. Stout and Bultman are staff consultants in the Visual Arts Program of the Fine Arts Work Center.

New Yorkers *William Freed* (1902–   ) and *Lillian Orlowsky* (1914–   ) enrolled in the Hofmann School when it was small and not yet popular. Hofmann came to rely on Freed's skill in setting up the still-life arrangements from which students were to draw when he was class monitor. Freed's precise command of structures was demonstrated when he built, by his own hand, his two-story house in a woodsy part of the East End, adding at its center a meticulously designed spiral staircase. In the cubist manner (it was basic to Hofmann's early teaching), Freed often demonstrates his command over a cascade of color planes. But in an alternative style he can also evoke surprise and a certain drama through the release of an impetuous brush and the delight in the accidental behavior of smoldering colors. As Hofmann, himself speaking of his own bouts with chance, has said: "For this you have to be in the rarest states."

In her collages, Lillian Orlowsky (Mrs. Freed) mingles opulent patterns for effects of mystery and complexity. Her alter ego is given to ink drawings from still life, impressions swiftly set down with knowing economy by a spirited brush.

Such early students as *Mercedes Carles* (Matter) and later, *Perle Fine* (1908–   ), extracted complex dynamism from their drawings of the model. The points at which forces seemed to intersect were indicated by criss-crossing lines suggesting many-layered, almost galactic spaces. Later when she made a liberating break with Cubism, Perle Fine explored giant organic forms and images derived from free association, her canvases were always too large to be accepted at the Art Association. Her ready grasp of Hofmann's theories on push and pull, the meeting and clashes of energies in space (the space surrounding the model), gave her a role as interpreter to bewildered members of the classes. She said that she has continued this "translation" over the years. After a productive decade in Provincetown, she left around 1955. Her husband, photographer and painter Maurice Berezov, studied with both Hawthorne and Hofmann. He found Hofmann "densely Germanic and scientific" after the experience in 1922 of working out-of-doors under the direction of Hawthorne (albeit in a class of around 300) whom Berezov saw as "inspiring and commanding."

The abstract painting of *Judith Rothschild* (1922–) is rooted in concepts that were being explored and amplified during the years following the end of World War II when, as a young girl, she first came to Provincetown. She studied with Hofmann for a season and, as a close friend of Karl Knaths, she also became deeply interested in his method of relating spatial and color intervals in painting to intervals in musical compositions. The abstract thinking of both artists supplemented influential concepts already encountered through personal contacts with Jean Arp, Fernand Leger, Joan Miro and other distinguished European artists. She found Hofmann "open, humble and beautiful." He was interested in the constructivist ideas of the Europeans, and teacher and student carried on "a real dialogue." In 1947 she was married to poet and writer, Tony Myrer, from a Portuguese family long established in Provincetown. They bought a property — an old net-mending shack on a wharf — opposite the Hofmanns. As a friend of Weldon Kees, she was involved in the continuous leg-work for Forum '49; her painting for the exhibition was an interplay of flowing and angular shapes based on city forms. In the 1950's she and her husband spent winters in Big Sur and other California locales, returning to Provincetown in the summer. Her grounding in classic constructivism prevented her from joining the drift to the automatism and loose gestural styles of that decade. Since her divorce and remarriage, Rothschild has lived summers in Wellfleet.

From the mid-1930's until very recently *Peter Busa* (1914–) was Provincetown's "stormy petrel" — conspicuously talented, vital and accomplished, also volatile in temperament, never long at home in any group. During the time of the WPA projects he knew Motherwell and Baziotes, and participated in some of the earliest experiments with automatism. He also had a one man show in 1946 at Peggy Guggenheim's Gallery, but he could not maintain a close relationship even with these innovating rebels and he is only now beginning to be mentioned in the early annals of the New York School. Today he writes from his new home in Southampton: "Busa was always an independent!"

He was first brought to Provincetown as a child (in 1916) by his parents who were friends of a local artist, Raymond Simboli, from Pittsburgh who had studied with Hawthorne. He returned to enter Hofmann's summer class in 1936 after having studied with him at the Art Students League in New York. He was included in the important Exhibition 200 in connection with Forum '49, and in the 1950's was a founding member of the cooperative Gallery 256 which was a successful group enterprise for two years. The third year his family took over the gallery following a lawsuit over the lease. In association with designer Ruth Reeves, he started a school at 149 Commercial called The Provincetown Art Center. During the 1960's Walter Chrysler was a liberal patron and gave Busa a retrospective exhibition in the later part of the decade.

From his large house and studio on Commercial Street in the East End, he produced series of outsized canvases in a style of broad divisions of space that changed from fluid and painterly to near geometric. Recently there has been renewed interest in his early paintings inspired by American Indian art.

When he was turning out his large, dynamically stroked, black-dominated abstractions in the 1950's, *Steven Pace* (1918–) said they often reflected shapes and movements, even sounds and smells recollected from his childhood on a farm in the Mid-West. Studies with Hofmann did not alter the associative elements in his work. In the early years in Provincetown when he was "roughing it" in a primitive shack on the dunes, his abstractions were stimulated by the wild surroundings; later, when his studio was in town, his abstract paintings were sometimes inspired by the reflections under the pier that fascinated him on his evening walks by the harbor.

In the early 1960's Pace turned away from abstraction and from his black calligraphy; possibly encouraged by the example of his friend, Milton Avery, he began to paint recognizable elements in the scene around him. From the overall attack with a fast moving brush — whites of the canvas flickering between criss-crossing strokes — materializes a pasture with horses, or in others a house, "Model T" car, one or two figures, earthy but shimmering in the light of Provincetown or Maine.

In the post war years *John Grillo* (1917–   ) considered himself an Abstract Expressionist though with no strong ideological commitment; he was already confident in the handling of the loose, painterly style and had influenced Hultberg, Diebenkorn and David Park during an extended stay in California just before he came to Provincetown in 1949. He studied with Hofmann (was class monitor) for most of two summers. Away from the Cape in 1951 and through 1954, on his return he was given a one-man show in the small shop of jeweler and painter, Earl Pilgrim. It aroused considerable interest though he was too poor at the time to buy canvas and had painted on all sorts of found materials including shingles and pieces of bark. His abstractions were composed as fields of glowing color — often yellows laced with jewel-like blues and oranges. He was invited to show at the HCE and later at the East Coast Gallery.

His style has changed a number of times — including a hardedge and a figurative phase — since 1962, the last summer he was in Provincetown. Today his teaching at Amherst is still based on Hofmann's concepts. Grillo says: "The more I thought I was going against him the more I was really going with him — and I learned so much. I realize it more and more. It was like a son going against a father."

"Provincetown was the greatest place in the world for me at that time," said *Warren Brandt* (1918–   ), a Southerner (from North Carolina, he was then head of the Art Department of the University of Mississippi). He was speaking of the summers of 1957 to 1959, when he rigged up a ramshackle studio from charred boards and items he found on the dump in a wild area full of lily ponds near the dunes in the West End. Having embraced Abstract Expressionism on his own via De Koonings he saw in New York, now he found himself in the company of artists who shared his enthusiasm and the excitement of new points of view. He remembered the Californians Ernest Briggs and Edward Dugmore, William Opper, Ed Corbett, Mary and Robert Frank and Dody Müller; and Steve Pace living in pioneer simplicity in a shack on the dunes. Brandt painted "like a maniac," without subject matter but incorporating among strokes of a liberated brush, the light and color of lily ponds and the feel of "broken down old docks." Following his marriage to Grace Borgenicht, the couple returned in the summers of 1961 and 1962, and he took over the large boat-builder's barn that had been Kline's studio. He was given a one-man show at the Esther Stuttman Gallery in 1962.

Lila Katzen (1932–   ) came from Baltimore to study with Hans Hofmann in 1948 and 1949. In 1952 she returned, rented a barn on Allerton Street and began painting on her own. By the later 1950's she had developed an abstract gestural style of cascading paint sometimes set off by metallic silver. Her drive to project forms beyond the boundaries of a frame had led her by the next decade into composing with movable overlays of transparent plastic or lucite with light streaming through to reveal organic, often plant-like forms (Miro has been her most constant influence). Walter Chrysler acquired several of these "light works." Subsequently she moved into the field of abstract metal sculpture and has produced some on a monumental scale — one is installed on the terrace of the Everson Museum. For decades her house and studio on Allerton Street have served as a permanent summer base. She writes: "I feel that I developed and grew in the time I spent in Provincetown. I met all the people from New York on a more lasting basis since I lived in Baltimore then (a teacher at the Maryland Institute College of Art), and relied on brief visits to New York."

In her year-round home on Anthony Street, *Marit Jensen* has assembled an interesting collection of her own works in painting and collage and also works by a number of distinguished colleagues she has known in over thirty seasons in Provincetown. She came in 1945 to study with Hofmann and returned to classes for ten summers. In her collages in which blacks often dominate, lines and angular shapes maintain a staccato rhythm with dynamic shifts in space implied in the interstices. An opposite mood is notable in her paintings — usually luminous interiors where one or two surprising accents contrast with softly brushed colors. Her works have been shown at Gallery 256, the New Gallery, Zabriskie Gallery, and the Wellfleet Gallery, and recently at the Group Gallery.

Through the teaching and painting of *Toni La Selle* (c. 1902–   ), Hofmann's concepts have been widely disseminated in Texas beginning with her native Denton. She found confirmation in Hofmann's teaching for a principle of color movement toward which she had been groping for years. Single-mindedly she pursued this idea in studies with Hofmann beginning in the 1940's and continuing in her independent work during summers in Provincetown for several decades. Her geometrically-patterned paintings have been widely exhibited in the South and have appeared in national exhibitions. She is a staff consultant and artist-in-residence at the Fine Arts Work Center.

Giorgio Cavallon (1904–   ) studied with Hawthorne in 1929, with Hofmann in 1935–1936. The simplified spatial divisions of his abstractions may indicate some debt to the Hofmann outlook, and "ghosts" of nature images abound in his work. But he has gone his own way. Perhaps it is because he is so finely attuned to light — as reflected in his inimitable off-whites — that he returns each year for part of the summer and lives by the harbor front. Along with sketching (sometimes in the cemetery) he devotes himself to fishing, preparing delicacies for old friends and, most ardently of all, to turning out a fine batch of beach plum jelly.

One of the most authoritative abstract painters in Provincetown, *Nassos Daphnis* (1914–   ) was entirely self-taught; born in Greece, this one-time primitive evolved his own color theory — symbolic and mathematical — and proceeded with quiet self-confidence to refine it through a series of geometric variations. When he first came (around 1955) and took a midtown apartment near the harbor, his canvases were based on a grid of rectangular modules; later he moved into compositions based on horizontal divisions, then into arcs and diamond-like shapes. Black which he uses as a frontal plane is equated with birth, blue with childhood; the adolescent and adult spans of life are expressed in different reds; old age in yellow. White is death. Translated into gleaming epoxy, his hard-edged arcs could be taken for minimalist, but only at first glance. After longer acquaintance they assume an icon-like intensity.

His work has had wide exposure: at Gallery 256, at the HCE Gallery and at Tirca-Karlis, as well as consistently in the Art Association. Yet in the modest house with adjoining studio he bought in the East End he finds the privacy he needs. He writes of Provincetown: "one can relax and be away from the crowd, to work and contemplate either by the dunes or by the water."

When *Helen Frankenthaler* (1928–   ) joined the Provincetown classes of Hans Hofmann at the suggestion of Clement Greenberg, the disciplines of Cubism were already familiar through intensive work at Bennington College with Paul Feeley and later study with Wallace Harrison. She responded to Hofmann as a teacher, and she was already preparing to take leave of Cubism. Moved by the late fluid improvisations of Arshile Gorky, even more deeply affected by extended visits (in company with Greenberg) to Jackson Pollock's studio in Springs, she was impelled to abandon the implicit grid of her earlier work and venture into a more open space in painting.

By the time she had returned to Provincetown as the wife of Robert Motherwell (they were married in 1958), she was in command of a technique that effectively corresponded to her concept of painting and drawing as a single process. As with Pollock, the painting support (usually unsized cotton duck) was laid out on the floor horizontally, requiring an athletic agility of the artist. But instead of his viscous skeins of enamel that thickened on the surface, Frankenthaler poured puddles of thinned pigment that soaked into the fabric support and merged into the ragged stains that finally emerged as components of a total image.

In many ways the surroundings of Provincetown entered into the imagery of her paintings. Clues to association with outward realities can be found in the pictures as well as in the titles: once the numbers "175" (the address of Robert Motherwell's house) could be discerned among slashing strokes. Easily identified with the surging rhythm of the sea or the monolithic presence of the dunes, even without the titles, are fluid shapes produced with poured paint through the twist of a wrist or sweep of the arm.

As a young painter and teacher, *Jan Gelb* (1906–   ) came to Provincetown in 1935 to work close to the dunes and sea on her lyric watercolors and oils of dreamlike images initiated through spontaneous doodles. After her marriage, she shared her dune hideaway with *Boris Margo* (1902–   ). At the first midsummer full moon the entire colony converged on the spot (in response to an invitation posted in the local newspaper) to roast their basket-party fare over layered bonfires rising more than 20 feet high by the shore.

A strong Slavic temperament (born in Wolotschisk, Russia), Margo had been influenced by Filonov, a Russian proto-Surrealist whose work is in the Hermitage. In Provincetown in the 1940's, Margo was developing his more abstract Surrealism at the time he opened a popular school on the dunes; later the school and Margo's own residence were transferred to the town. A new stage in his work was inaugurated in the 1950's through his intense interest in calligraphy ranging from Chinese to primitive and Hebraic. Extremely simplified compositions — often sanded variations of whites — were built around his own embossed or recessed versions of written characters; they also appeared on shaped canvases. In his recent paintings this calligraphy, constantly in transformation, comprises delicate bands afloat in airy, pale-toned spaces.

From the West Coast contingent of abstract painters — with strong ties to Abstract Expressionism — came *Edward Corbett* (1919–1971) in the early 1960's. (Californians Dugmore and Briggs were in Provincetown in the late 1950's.) Before his death in Provincetown in 1971, he had produced a distinguished series inspired by the landscape of the Cape End — those with "Provincetown" in the title number from 1 to 49. After serving in World War II, he had been invited to teach at the California School of Fine Arts by Douglas MacAgy. There he came to know Clyfford Still as "a fighter and a man of real spirit;" in spite of his own deep influence from Mondrian he agreed with Still's call for a symbolic break with European influence. On a trip to New York he met Ad Reinhardt who said later that Corbett's painting led him to see the possibilities of black in his own work. In 1962 he married Rosamond Tirana; based in Washington, she summered on the Cape. In spite of worsening health (an amputated leg and complications) he was working at his best, the landscape reflected in subtle changes in his style. His earlier abstractions suggested landscapes seen from a plane with delicate fissure lines and softly broken planes barely flushed with color. On the Cape his work was still composed of multiple thin films of paint but color was often more luminous and planes more constructed. Corbett never changed his conviction that the artist's visual surroundings have an inescapable effect on his work. After an earlier experience he had said: "I believe my first moments of significant self awareness of imaginative life were when I became speculatively involved with the dramatic nature around me ... "

Living year round in Provincetown since the early 1950's, *Jim Forsberg* (1919–   ) was familiar with the abstract approaches of Hofmann through earlier study with Cameron Booth, himself a student at Hofmann's school in Munich. A luxuriant, almost opulent range of color has been important in both his fauvishly realist and abstract phases. He returns again and again, with variations on rhythmically disposed shapes, to the inside-outside spatial play of the window theme. In a recent development with symbolic overtones, the window grill was a foil for looming spheres of metallic gold.

Forsberg is a staff consultant of the Fine Arts Work Center; he is proprietor of the indispensable (for artists' materials) Studio Shop.

A summer resident since 1945, *Ian Pinkerson* (1913–   ) is extremely active in the affairs of the colony from her home in the West End. Following study with Hofmann her work remained semi-abstract: a psychological element is projected through dreamlike images of the sea. Her husband, the late Harry Pinkerson, was president of the Provincetown Art Association.

In the abstractions of *Edward Giobbi* (1926–   ) the radiant light that was the focus of his studies with Henry Hensche — "light bouncing off things" — becomes an ambience for machine-like forms inspired by the Italian Futurists. Giobbi studied with Henry Hensche in Provincetown in the summers of 1948 and 1949. The following year, in an extended study trip to Italy, land of his forbearers, he was deeply influenced by Futurism although his work remained realist. Returning to Provincetown in the mid-1950's, he bought a house and was a summer resident until 1965, showing his work at the Shore Gallery, and with groups at the HCE. In a series of one-man shows at Tirce Karlis, a kinetic element — the surface agitated by repeated, often brick-like patterns — became increasingly important in his abstractions. Recognizable images appeared in an abstracted, film-like sequence in a large painting dealing with the Kennedy assassination.

Abstract Expressionists

They did not come in a body or carrying a banner — the artists later called Abstract Expressionists, "Action Painters," and members of the New York School. They arrived one by one and at different times: in the late 1930's *Arshile Gorky* came on extended visits, cooked Armenian delicacies for his friends and lectured on Picasso's symbolism. *Jackson Pollock, Adolph Gottlieb* and *William Baziotes* arrived early, just before and after the end of World War II; *Mark Rothko* several years later and then, very late, *Franz Kline* around 1957, *Robert Motherwell* in and out for years and then to stay after 1958. Not one of them had studied with Hofmann (although Lee Krasner, Pollock's wife, had been his student), but if there was any constant relationship it was with Hofmann, informally they became a part of the milieu of his circle.

How different they were: Pollock tempestuous and unpredictable; Baziotes wrapped in his inner dream; Gottlieb the extrovert, a bronzed sportsman, consistent winner of the boat racing events; college trained, intellectually keen Motherwell and Kline alternating hard work with hard play, the latter the idol of his night-spot companions. Provincetown accentuated divergencies in their backgrounds. Russian-born Rothko and Gottlieb had known each other since youth, both had felt the pressures of intense and bookish Jewish families; together they had become disciples of Milton Avery. But on the Cape, Rothko

74

lacked his friend's sporting way of relating to this environment. He remained a city boy out of his element. Greek-born Baziotes, who should have been at home near the sea and whose paintings evoked a sub-marine world, was miserable at the beach (partly because of frail health). It was in the studio that he made small pastels and watercolors — the first stages of his larger recreations of the unseen. During the years when these four had been getting to know each other on the WPA projects, Motherwell was learning how to think about the history of art from Professor Meyer Schapiro at Columbia University. Franz Kline, born into a Pennsylvania Dutch family in Wilkes Barre, was traveling an opposite road into the art world. In the early 1930's he had come to Provincetown and studied with Hawthorne's assistant, Henry Hensche — he always acknowledged Hensche as his teacher. After studies at the Heatherly Art School in England (returning with an English bride), he was a designer of theatrical scenery and worked for department stores. He showed his work at the Washington Square Outdoor Show in 1939. At a time when the future Abstract Expressionists were being discovered by Peggy Guggenheim, Kline was being awarded prizes at the National Academy Annual. While Gottlieb and Rothko were exploring surrealism, involved with mythic themes and primitive art, Kline was painting quick-sketch portraits and cabaret subjects in downtown bars.

Provincetown saw each of them at different stages of their careers. Pollock's longest documented stays, the summers of 1943 and 1944, coincided with his first substantial recognition (he was commissioned by Peggy Guggenheim to paint a twenty-foot mural for her entrance hall in 1943). His open space, all-over frieze of frenzied figural images was created with a swinging brush — the first drip painting still four years in the future (there are conflicting reports of what he produced in Provincetown).

Pollock (1912–1956) came those summers with his wife, Lee Krasner. When they visited the Hofmanns, Pollock needled the teacher relentlessly for his reluctance to exhibit his work: if he did not show, he was not a painter. Their heated talks continued at every meeting. Afterwards Hofmann bought a painting by Pollock, and plans went forward for a 1944 show of Hofmann's paintings at Peggy Guggenheim's *Art of this Century Gallery* in New York. It proved to be a turning point, the beginning of Hofmann's return to the art world as a painter.

In an exact clockwork schedule Gottlieb (1903–1974) painted in the mornings, sailed afternoons. When he came to Provincetown around 1944, Gottlieb was still engrossed in his "pictograph" paintings with grid-like compartments containing stylized, symbolic motifs: eyes, suns, arrows, genitals. His interest was not in their specific references but in their evocation of the pre-logical expression of primitive peoples and archaic cultures — a search for timeless universals that obsessed most of the group at this time. A passing interest in myths of American Indians was replaced by themes from classic mythology, then finally with figurations thought of as having cosmic implications. Progressive simplifications led him, by 1951, to a canvas divided by a horizon into two parts. The emblems — now simple spheres and lozenge-like rectangles — appear in the sky area; some of the older pictographic symbols have a subterranean life in the rough brushwork of the earth half. This focus on duality was to lead him by 1958, when he was taking leave of the Cape, to the "bursts" that were to occupy him for much of the rest of his life. He died in 1974. Gottlieb and Baziotes found a supportive dealer in Sam Kootz but prices were low and sales few in the 1940's. In 1954 Gottlieb was given a one man show at the Kootz Gallery in Provincetown. It was in his modest waterfront studio that Gottlieb designed and tested the stained glass panels of his facade for the Milton Steinberg Memorial.

By the time the colony was getting used to the flashier life style of a newly successful Abstract Expressionist — with the arrival around 1957 of Franz Kline

Franz Kline's House and Studio, Provincetown

— a great deal had happened and the center of the international art world was shifting to New York. In 1956 Jackson Pollock had sold a painting for an unprecedented $30,000; later in that same year he was killed while driving recklessly.

Kline (1910–1962) had once told a New York audience that whereas Thoreau was always worrying about the noise on the road to Boston, he, Kline wanted to be a part of that noise. Now he was in Thoreau country and very conspicuous on Commercial Street in his red Maserati always driven by Mike Welsh (not because Kline wanted the luxury of a chauffeur but because he was such a terrible driver, especially when he had been drinking, that he was not permitted at the wheel). An attractive man still in his forties, he was described by an admirer as "a sawed-off Ronald Coleman." While he was far from rich from the sales of his large black and white abstractions at the Sidney Janis Gallery — he was also deeply in debt for the medical expenses of his institutionalized English wife — he could barely afford the unusually designed, grove-shaded house he bought in the West End and the one-time boat house nearby that had been Jackson Pollock's studio.

The dynamism of Kline's gestural abstractions — by then attracting national and international attention — made him seem the pure example of the "action painter" whose legend of boldness and impetuosity excited curiosity as to the performance. The visitors who were invited — rarely — to his studio were sometimes surprised to see designs sketched in charcoal on a newly stretched canvas — an absolute heresy to the dogma that the method was direct and unstudied, the painting "an arena for action." To his close friends it was no secret that the sweeping black and white shapes were often invented enlargements from small studies, the method a possible relic of the early pressing need to conserve canvas. His use of quick-drying and inexpensive house painter's enamels had also originally been dictated by need.

It was exhausting work, these days and weeks of adjustment — often through quick, sweeping wipes with a turpentine-soaked rag — of his giant, thrusting blacks and whites so that neither would be a background for the other. To relax afterwards he drank under the trees with his driver and gardener. After dark it was Reggie Cabral's Atlantic House, then in its heyday; in its live jazz bands one might spot the painter, Howard Kanowitz, or Larry Rivers, a one-time student in the Hofmann classes, on saxophone.

In the summer of 1962 Kline flew to Italy to accept an award for his painting in the U.S. Pavilion at the Venice Biennale. Soon after his return he died of a heart attack. He was fifty-one.

About a decade later than his first sojourn in 1948, *Mark Rothko* (1903–1970) returned to Provincetown and bought a modest house pleasantly situated off Bradford Street in the East End with adequate space for a studio. In the interval all traces of surrealist imagery had disappeared from his work. His concept was stunningly simple and seldom varied: two or three atmospheric shapes of opulent but off-beat color vibrantly brushed into the unsized canvas so as to echo the rectangle of the canvas and appear to hover within it. Several years later they would comprise the bulk of his important exhibition at the Musuem of Modern Art. But his plan for relaxed summers collided with a series of mural commissions, the first for the Four Seasons Restaurant from which he ultimately withdrew the finished paintings. From this time his paintings became more severe in format, more somber in color with a dominance of the blacks which he himself said, in a 1958 talk, indicated a preoccupation with death.

For several seasons he rented his house to Expressionist painter, Maurice Sievan, then in 1965 he sold it to Tony and Elspeth Vevers, young artists to whom he was sympathetic.

Rothko was a deeply disturbed and bitter man when he came, again, to rented quarters and studio in the East End in the summer of 1969. He was rich and internationally acclaimed, but, as his friend Stanley Kunitz observed, he was consumed by the shift of the art world spotlight to other artists, some of whom he felt were influenced by his work. In a gesture that his friends regarded hopefully, he invited a group of young painters to visit him at his studio on a weekly basis for an informal exchange of views. His first exploration of painting with acrylics was another reason for encouragement. In a series of small studies on paper he seemed to be recovering the glowing color of his early work.

It was Rothko's hope initially that when he returned to the city he would be able to develop new large-scale paintings based on the summer's studies. But even before he left Provincetown he was in a mood of deep gloom. The meetings with young artists had proved unrewarding; he said he did not care what they were thinking about. Back in the city his work became darker and more severe in the early winter months. He adopted a horizontal format with the canvas divided almost equally into fields of black above and greyed ochers in the lower half; that became, by association, a foreboding sky and desolate earth. On February 15, 1970, he took his life.

When he came to the Cape in the early 1920's, *Jack Tworkov* (1900–   ) was already familiar with the Impressionist approach to painting through classes with Hawthorne at the National Academy; in still lifes and figure compositons he was developing his own sensitive style of simplified forms and muted colors. In Provincetown he studied for a summer with Ross Moffett. He has a vivid recollection of John Noble at the Beachcombers. When Moffett took him to the studio of Karl Knaths he was deeply impressed by the artist and interested in his semi-abstract work.

Having emigrated with his family from Poland when he was an adolescent, young Tworkov, serious and searching by temperament and widely read in the classics, felt a need to integrate the experience of growing up in the old world culture with the everyday reality of life in New York. During the years of the Depression and of work on the WPA (easel) projects, he saw himself as pushed off course by economic and political pressures. Later his job in wartime industry afforded neither time for painting nor for a return to Provincetown.

He felt as though a stone were being rolled off his back after the war when it was again possible to turn to the private concerns and inner-directed life that for him was a condition for creativity. Psychoanalysis, with its revelation of the role of the unconscious in art, seemed enormously promising in the light of the spontaneous techniques being explored by DeKooning and others. Tworkov experimented with automatism and at the same time continued cubistically simplified still life paintings.

By 1955 when Jack and his wife, Wally, returned to Provincetown and settled there (following an initial exploration that unexpectedly showed much of the cherished landscape intact), he had developed his authoritative style of feathering brush strokes — reds and blues alternating with misty yellows, white and pinks — set down in superimposed layers. Tworkov's large abstractions were shown at the HCE Gallery and often at the Art Association.

In 1958 the Tworkovs bought a pleasant old house set back by a sweep of lawn from Commercial Street at the extreme West End (next door to Stanley Kunitz and Elise Asher and a stone's throw from the wooded acres of the Knath's home and studio). Living in Provincetown five or six months of the year, working in the well-lighted studio that he added himself, on paintings that are now geometrically structured and composed of free-form modules, he swims almost daily and waits for the fall when he can walk in the woods and dunes. "But as an abstract painter," he said, "the pictures come out pretty much the same in New York as in Provincetown."

In 1956 just as Adolph Gottlieb was getting ready to make his move to more affluent Easthampton, *Robert Motherwell* (1915–   ) who had long divided his loyalty between the Cape and Long Island — as had Kline, Rothko and Baziotes — bought an 18th-century house and settled in Provincetown. Among the original Abstract Expressionists, Motherwell has proved a strikingly durable figure, more flexible than his early colleagues, less bent on pure and universal solutions. His work, in fact, occupies a fertile middle ground between the gestural power identified with Jackson Pollock and the sustained painterly fields of Mark Rothko and Clyfford Still. In the development of this synthesis he was prodded by another mixed means: the collage combined with painting that was to continue to occupy him in Provincetown.

In an interview conducted by Budd Hopkins before a general audience at the Fine Arts Work Center in the summer of 1976, Motherwell recalled a time when, facing surgery of doubtful outcome, he had produced one of his most joyous paintings. In describing his work he repeatedly used the word "passion;" he said his work was deeply emotional in motivation and execution. The emphasis was surprising to some who assumed that for the sophisticated style of this scholar in contemporary art (he had edited an anthology on *The Dada Painters and Poets,* published by Wittenborn and Schultz, New York, and also, with Ad Reinhardt, an anthology of *Modern Artists in America*), a more cerebral approach was to be expected. Certainly Motherwell's art historical perspectives must have helped him deal with changes in the art world: unlike Rothko who was consumed with self-destructive anger when the focus of attention shifted from Abstract Expressionism to new styles, Motherwell greeted the appearance of Pop Art with expressions of genial interest.

After his marriage to Helen Frankenthaler in 1958, Motherwell bought adjoining houses in the extreme East End on the harbor side with ample space for their separate studios. After an initial period of travels abroad they settled into spending most of the summers at work in their studios overlooking the bay. In 1962 Motherwell said that he mainly used color symbolically: ocher for the earth, green for the grass, blue for the sky and sea. Blue was the most important color in an extended series he began that summer, all oil on rag paper and all titled *Beside the Sea,* with numerals added. The theme is evoked by horizontal sweeps of the brush below spray-like spatters of paint.

Paul Burlin (1886–1969) lived long enough to regard the different periods in his life as "dynasties;" with his undiminished appetite for experience, he was bound to plunge into the life of different colonies — three are documented and maybe more. He must have been an asset to all of them — his caustic wit always aimed at mediocrity — but in the case of his first venture, to Santa Fe in 1913, his pioneering as a painter was memorable. He showed that the arts of primitive peoples — in this case the Pueblo Indians — could be tapped not just for picturesque effects or decorative motifs: the point was to appropriate its vital underlying rhythms.

Burlin was in Provincetown for most summers in the late 1950's and early 1960's. He usually rented a studio in the row above Days Lumberyard and in spite of vision badly impaired by cataracts, produced some of his strongest work. In the midst of the jostling color planes of his large abstractions — smudged and smokey hues alongside sharp ones — certain of the chunky irregular shapes were still associated with things seen and heard. He would tease his dinner guests to identify them.

George McNeil (1908–   ) was the opposite of a colony-hopper. He was repelled by the social life of the colony, regarded the round of parties and openings as "an abomination." Of all the Abstract Expressionists he was the most outspokenly moved by the natural beauty of the Cape End. But McNeil rarely painted landscape. He had studied with Hofmann in New York in the late

1930's and, with Mercedes Carles and Wilfred Zogbaum, had become part of a group of close friends of the teacher. His abstractions with their rich impasto and sandy textures, usually began in the Hofmannesque way with drawing and painting from the model. He came with his wife, Dora, in 1948. After working in one of Days studios for a year or two, he moved into a house in the East End where he maintained a disciplined routine and turned out an impressive body of work until he left after the summer of 1963. He remembers how, before the place became tourist-plagued, each year he would feel "rejuvenated by the first experience of the clean brilliance of the sand against sea and sky — as if that pure sensation had swept away the debris of city living."

Galleries

Beginning around 1957 and continuing for about a decade it was often possible to see as much distinguished American art in eight or ten galleries on Commercial Street as one could making the rounds of 57th Street and Madison in New York on a typical Saturday afternoon (the total count of galleries, including those devoted to crafts and novelties, varies from 24 to 32).

On Friday evenings when most galleries opened a new show in the 1960's, groups of the local intelligentsia — dressed as colorfully as possible and wearing their most dramatic jewelry — usually began the gala tour around nine o'clock at the picturesque East End Gallery. Then, on foot of course, down to the posh HCE and on to a half dozen more stops — sampling the wine and greeting friends all along the way. Until 1959 a stop at the Sun Gallery could involve a poetry reading, with seating on the floor, in any case always a surprising change from the elegance of the HCE.

Approaching Midtown it was time to join an animated throng down the Mews to the Group Gallery (after 1965), then time for a rest on the yellow bench outside the door of Tirca-Karlis before a tour of her upstairs and downstairs offerings. If the Chrysler Museum had an opening, one dashed across the street to join an even larger crowd before pressing on to the Cafe Poyant for refreshment and a look-in at the gallery under the Art Cinema (256, The New Gallery, then East Coast Gallery). Hardy souls expected to make it before eleven to the Kessler Gallery at the extreme West End and, for a season, to Zabriskie.

Some wound up at Reggie Cabral's "A" House (Atlantic House) for drinks, a good jazz band and free style dancing. Collectors sometimes joined the Friday night trek but they then retired to the gracious comfort of the Seascape Hotel or Colonial Inn (now both gone) and returned the following day for hard bargaining.

Because it was stimulating, socially enjoyable and for some quite profitable, the market place flourished in Provincetown over more than a decade. It was a grievous affront to a minority of older artists who saw the multiplication of galleries as fostering a hectic and competitive way of life, a violation of the solitude essential for creation.

If this commercialism was a betrayal of the ideal of what this place should be, it is hard to find the villain. Galleries were a logical growth of Provincetown's organizationally active life; they also reflected the "culture boom" in New York. The Art Association itself had proven very successful in selling members' paintings; the proprietor of the first large gallery, the Shore Gallery, was Donald Witherstine, a former officer of the association. After Forum '49, with its successful exhibitions and debates that extended over a summer, the possibilities of Provincetown as a showcase for the artist were very clear.

The early cooperatives were inspired by aesthetic causes and generous intentions; neither they nor the Sun Gallery (supported by a proprietor who washed dishes to afford it) were big commercial enterprises.

Sun Gallery 1956–1959

Occupying what was surely the smallest gallery space in town (25 by 16 feet), the Sun Gallery became a haven for vital mavericks; it offered a focus for all the volatile energies and ideas that were excluded from the established coteries. The shows and events crowded into its four years were sometimes comic and improvised, sometimes poetic or dramatic, at other times rough, raucous and deliberately crude. They were nearly always surprising and very often involved some participation of viewers. Some of the main art movements of the 1960's were forecast at the Sun Gallery.

Before it was the Sun, the miniscule space was occupied by an imaginative jeweler, Earl Pilgrim, who received a surprising response when he invited Wolf Kahn and John Grillo, both outstanding students of Hans Hofmann, to exhibit some of their paintings. This was at a time when it was unheard of for budding talents to be exhibited. In 1955 painter Yvonne Anderson who had been frustrated in a brief stint at the Hofmann School, joined with poet Dominick Falcone to take over the then vacant gallery space as a gallery for generally young, innovating artists. They had no help from grants or other sources in financing it; Falcone washed dishes at the Moors Restaurant to support the project. It was there that he met another dishwasher-artist with a shock of reddish-blond hair; they nicknamed him "Red" (Grooms) and invited him to join the Sun.

Anderson and Falcone were not out to make money or to promote some novel style. If they were exceptionally open to such innovations as happenings, events and assemblage art, it was because they had a hunch the time was ripe for a more informal, involving, even participating, relationship between artist and viewer (later Anderson called this "public art"). Yet straight painting of the figure or landscape was also appreciated if it was simplified and direct. Lester Johnson was given a one man show for paintings most often around the theme of a human profile and schematic plant form. A show of children's art signaled the approved immediacy with paint. Allan Kaprow who had already inaugurated "proto happenings" in New York was given a one man show. He also explored a score of different ways of handling a head (flat, built-up, cut-out, etc.) in a large assemblage called *Veronica's*.

The most loved, admired and imitated artist of the Sun Gallery was *Jan Müller;* even before his untimely death in 1958 from heart failure at the age of 38 he was a legend. Because he had succeeded in making the transition from an abstract to a symbolic expression, his painting opened doors for younger modern painters that had been resolutely shut for years. Born in Hamburg, Germany, December 27, 1922, Jan arrived in the U.S. in 1941 after eight years of wandering as a fugitive from Nazism. He had suffered two severe attacks of rheumatic fever.

Jan Müller was in Provincetown in the summers of 1950, 1951 and 1952. During five years of study with Hans Hofmann, a close — almost father-and-son — relationship grew up between the two German emigres; it was painful for both when, around 1951, Jan felt impelled to break with the abstract credo and to shift from his earlier mosaic-like abstract style to a painterly, expressionist mode with representational elements materialized from a flux of color spots. In 1955 he showed at the Sun Gallery a series of paintings of forest paths banded with light. His health was failing fast but the following year he married Dolores (Dody) James in Provincetown and that summer he painted a monumental series with figurative subjects drawn from myth and literature: *Of This Time-Of That Place, Hamlet and Horatio, Walpurgisnacht-Faust* I. From the Faust theme he moved more deeply into the bizarre medieval world peopled with grimacing white-masked witches and monstrous hexes. But even as they lose all reference to real landscape they are charged with energies reinforced by a play of opposites: the grim demonic images in joyous, singing colors, the romantic subject matter in a classic structure formed of abstract expressionist brushwork.

In the summer of 1957, in spite of an eight-week attack of rheumatic fever, he painted in Provincetown some of his greatest works: *The Concert of Angels, The Search for the Unicorn, Great Hanging Piece.* When a number of these were shown that summer at the Sun Gallery it was clear that in his breakthrough from abstraction Jan Müller had arrived at something very different from DeKooning. In 1954 Müller had undergone unsuccessful surgery for replacement of his damaged heart valve with a plastic one that caused painful seizures. He died in January 1958, a month after becoming a United States citizen. Among those who were influenced by Jan Müller was *Bob Thompson* (1937–1966), a talented black artist who was also to die tragically young, and *Tony Vevers* (born in England, a year-round resident since 1955). In his 1958 one-man show at the Sun one of the most striking paintings portrayed Vevers' memory of the funeral of Jan Müller attended by his fellow artists, with the sun breaking through the snow-covered trees of the North Truro Cemetery. It was bought by Joseph Hirshhorn. Vevers' style was softer, more gently lyrical than Müller's; even in his powerful *Allegory* the quartet of nudes menaced by a dark force are still luminously palpable and the shore behind them mistily believable.

The Sun Gallery was the liveliest and also the most controversial gallery in town. Visitors were charmed when they were invited in to sit on the floor for poetry readings by Dom Falcone (his verses were often in the gallery window).

But at least one show at the Sun in the late fifties was deeply disturbing both because of its brutal subject theme and the deliberate crudeness of execution. This was *The City* conceived as a total environment with alternately two- and three-dimensional sections by Anderson, Johnson and Grooms. A grim mood was projected by blocky buildings, some in flames, with lumbering trucks and particularly by the figures shaped roughly by Anderson of tar over chicken wire. The large scale heightened the impact of a scene that was fearful yet presented without metaphor or drama. This was as far as possible removed from the romantic and idealized scene so long popular in Provincetown.

Surprising, at least to *Alex Katz* (1927–   ), was the outrage expressed by some viewers — they brandished fists from outside the windows — over some paintings of his in the window in his first show there. They were not the huge, poster-like images that have made him successful today; they included a flat simplified figure of his wife, Ada, and a collage of the lighthouse at the point. It was also a window display — a drawing of a dancing nude by Tony Vevers — that caused the police to descend on the gallery and close it for several days. After a petition containing the names of nearly every artist of prominence in the colony was presented to the police, the gallery was permitted to reopen.

"Magical stuff was going on (at the Sun Gallery)," said *Red Grooms* (1937–   ), "... it was the opposite of the abstract people, I blossomed under their influence." Grooms quit the Hofmann School two weeks after he met Falcone. "I didn't know how to appreciate Hofmann," he said. "I liked him but it was an academic scene, there were certain ways of doing everything." After the summer of 1957 Grooms shared a loft with Anderson and Falcone in New York while he worked as an usher at the Roxy movie house. They returned to Provincetown and to the Sun together, and at the end of the summer launched into a project that he said Yvonne Anderson thought of as proletarian — bringing art to the people. Outdoor billboards were to be used, not to advertise anything, but to show the paintings of Yvonne Anderson, Lester Johnson and Grooms. After more than a month's work their three huge paintings were mounted on telephone poles and erected on the edge of a parking lot owned by Falcone's father in Salisbury, Massachusetts. Grooms described his: "(I painted) two large long-legged figures walking in front of a parking lot on roller coasters — kind of a scene of a scene . . . " With a typical indifference to their works as precious art objects, they left them there to disintegrate.

Also indicating a "loose identity" and an "open attitude" was "a kind of play" conceived by Falcone and Anderson for two artists working in full public view. It was a performance that must have been intended as an ironic jibe at the exaggerated claim of the Abstract Expressionists to the uniqueness of the individual performance. With their heads covered by paper bags — holes punched for eyes — Grooms and Anderson established their anonymity, and further cancelled out their personal styles by crossing over into each other's work, as they painted on the same 6 foot wide canvas two grotesque heads, side by side but oddly different in size and character.

Later when Grooms tackled a performance — painting on his own "a play called *Fire*" — he felt he was "plunging into the unknown, something existential, just letting it happen," as he went to work on a horizontal canvas about seventeen feet wide before an audience seated on brown paper on the floor. Some angry sailors wandering in off the street almost spoiled the action. "It was the opposite of literary theater," he said, "rough, crude but stimulating."

In another unstructured "play" called *Walking Man* and presented twice each night after Labor Day 1959, Grooms was made up in white face with flour as "the pasty man." In the course of a noisy search he fell through a cardboard chute into a group of strikingly made up types (Anderson as a blind woman) emerging from a shadow play sequence with sound effects. Red had lots of encouragement in these impulses that summer. Lucas Samaris and Robert Whitman were briefly visitors; Allan Kaprow said: "You can do anything." It was the year that Kaprow himself first used the word "happening."

With the breaking up in the later 1950's of a number of the stylistic groupings, some fledgling artists were drawn to the Sun Gallery because they were aesthetically homeless. There were gifted Hofmann students ready to cut the umbilical cord and apply their newly-won painterly freedoms to the creation of recognizable images. In addition to Jan Müller, there was Bob Thompson, with a similarly fantastic imagery; Robert Beauchamp (1928–   ), also involved with themes of witches and demons, but in a more luxuriant milieu, and Wolf Kahn (1927–   ) who was forming landscapes from a luminous mesh of brushstrokes. John Grillo was developing an abstract field of radiant color, and Toni La Selle was channeling spatial color sensations into precise geometrical patterns. Several young artists were bent on exploring portraiture with a new directness, flatness and understated psychological angle: Marcia Marcus, Selina Trieff and Alex Katz, whose statement was above all, "cool." Human and plant silhouettes were equated symbolically in the subdued paintings of Lester Johnson. For Elise Asher, a poet as well as a visual artist, painting was handwriting — not one calligraphy but many, and superimposed mysteriously in layers that preserved the energy and changing rhythms of the fragments inscribed.

In 1959 when Yvonne Anderson and Dom Falcone had to give up the gallery for projects elsewhere, it was taken over by Bill Barrell who ran it in the same spirit. One of his most provocative exhibitions was of the cardboard and burnt-edged newspaper collages by Claes Oldenberg.

For a season or two all these diverse directions and temperaments were encompassed by the glow of the "magical things" and open perspectives that Falcone and Anderson invited. For a number of the artists, "art for art's sake" was replaced for a time by "art for people's sake," yet without any political ax to grind. The art objects exhibited could be rough and crude in execution as long as they were made to evoke an exchange, inspire a communication. Obviously the audience did not always appreciate this effort — often they were angered by the lack of polish and "beauty" in accustomed means. But those who "got the idea" remember the Sun vividly even now and wonder why it could not have lasted. A member of the gallery, Salvatore Del Deo, said: "The Sun Gallery did more for young artists than anyone else in the country."

Later, in the early 1960's, when work by some former Sun artists was being shown in small New York galleries, ideas and impulses, once fluid and playful, had hardened and become more programatic — a necessary phase but very different from the glow of exchange and exhilaration of discovery that had stirred fledgling artists at the Sun.

Gallery 256

When artists began to think seriously about showing and selling their work in Provincetown there was one gallery space that was particularly attractive because of its location at the very heart of the town's activities. This was 256 Commercial Street, a basement located under the movie house next door to the Town Hall, and it was approached via the popular Poyant outdoor restaurant. Over two decades it would house several quality galleries. In 1953 it was owned by Judge Robert Welsh who was willing to lease it for a token fee to a group eager to form the colony's first cooperative gallery. With John Frank as director, it included Peter Busa, Henry Botkin, Boris Margo, Leo Manso, Ruth Reeves, Robert Richenberg, Therese Schwartz and Myron Stout. They were different in style but for all of them abstraction was a cause, not only the earlier compass-and-ruler abstraction, but a freer idiom that could even embrace symbols. They needed a gallery because the large-scale work that was a must for some of them had brought exclusion from Art Association exhibitions.

In 1954 the group invited a number of other artists to join them in their July and August exhibitions: Ann Brigadier, Will Barnet, Victor Candell, Eve Clendenin, John Frank, Louise Nevelson, Hale Woodruf, Seong Moy, John von Wicht, Nassos Daphnis, Byron Browne, Lawrence Kupferman, Adja Yunkers, Richard Stankiewicz, Fredric Varady, Kenneth Campbell, Vivian de Pinna, Warren Brandt, Ian Pinkerson, Varujan Boghosian. The *Provincetown Advocate*, in covering their exhibition opening jammed with a crowd of 450, called it a "miniature Whitney Annual." They were encouraged by a daily attendance of 150 people.

In their July forum, called "The Young Artist Speaks," the group introduced an emphasis on the youthful artist that was subsequently to dominate the art world. (In earlier days of the colony, budding artists were expected to defer to their elders.) Questions about how abstract art should be interpreted ("as a unique personal gesture?") were fielded by panelists Nassos Daphnis, Allan Kaprow, Sam Spanier, Wolf Kahn, Steve Pace, and Mary Shaier. Myron Stout summed up: "A painting is generative, not reflective, substantial not vacuously transparent, above all it is a reality not an imitation or an illusion."

Gallery 256 reflected both the advantages of camaraderie and a spirit of cooperation with the difficulties of preserving it. Following a lawsuit over the lease, members of the cooperative lost the space which was taken over by the Busa family. For the summer of 1955 the artists were accepted into the fold of the HCE by Nat Halper; the following year they returned to the gallery at 256 Commercial, and exhibited there for two seasons. In 1958 the space was taken over by Martha Jackson as a summer extension of her New York Gallery with Steve Joy as director. Among the several local artists she included was Peter Busa.

At the end of the 1950's, when the space was agáin vacant, another cooperative under the name of *The New Gallery* was organized, with Bruno Palmer Poroner as director and Warren Brandt as president. Its founding artists,

Helen Avlon invited Vivian de Pinna, Ian Pinkerson, Neta Arias, Jehan Shaly (Samuels), Robert Henry, Arlie Sinaiko, John Grillo, Therese Schwartz and Selina Trieff.

From 1964 to 1969 this same space at 256 Commercial was occupied by a cooperative under the name *The East Coast Gallery* founded by Harvey Dodd, Nancy Brown, and Mildred Edinger, with Katherine Burnside as director (Burnside has won awards on the Cape and her work has been widely exhibited in the South).

Kootz-HCE

From 1953 to 1967 the gallery inaugurated by the New York dealer Samuel Kootz and later run by Nathan Halper (a Joyce scholar) as the HCE, was the showplace for the artist who had arrived. Those who had attracted favorable attention at Gallery 256 or the Sun Gallery might "graduate" to this attractively designed modern gallery not far from the Art Association in the East End. Its prestigious openings were not to be missed. In the early 1950's when Kootz was summering in a waterfront cottage owned by the painter Marjorie Windust and her husband, "Nat" Halper arranged to build a gallery on their property as part of a real estate exchange. In 1953 and 1954, he was able to give shows for his New York gallery members in Provincetown: Hofmann, Baziotes, Gottlieb, and also Motherwell, who was often there. He also showed work by Bultman, sculpture by David Hare and Ibraim Lassaw and (in 1954) some by Herbert Ferber.

As he found the operation of the Provincetown gallery taking too much time from his writing, Kootz turned over the gallery to Halper who initially called it the HC. He accepted the group who had exhibited at 256, and gave shows to Henry Botkin, Edwin Dickinson, Philip Malicoat, Bruce McKain, Fritz Bultman, Ann Brigadier and Loren MacIver. The following year Halper changed the name to HCE; he invited Victor Candell and Moy Engel. Subsequently Leo Manso, Louise Nevelson, Nassos Daphnis and Therese Schwartz returned to the gallery from 256. Also added were Conrad Malicoat and Rosalyn Drexler.

Featured in smaller displays during the twelve years of the HCE were drawings by Motherwell, lithographs by Gottlieb, drawings by Müller, Milton Avery; collages by Victor Candell, Ralph Rosenborg and Ann Brigadier, and works in various mediums by Nassos Daphnis, Tony Vevers, David Young, Marsden Hartley, Nanno de Groot, Angelo Ippolito, Steve Pace, George McNeil, Robert Beauchamp, Gandy Brodie, William Freed, Maurice Sievan, Edwin Dickinson and Philip Malicoat.

Among those represented by individual works were: Jack Tworkov, Robert Richenberg, Ronald Ting, Glen Wesselman, Peter Hutchinson, Fritz Varady, Lucas Samaris, Milton Resnick, Dick Klix, Alfred Leslie, Richard Florsheim, Lily Harmon, Selina Trieff, Jehan Shaly, Peter Watts, Myron Stout, William Opper, Dody Müller, Sherman Drexler, Karl Knaths, Ross Moffett, Jack Yeats, Howard Kanowitz, Felix Pasilis, Edward Dugmore, Ernest Briggs, Judith Rothschild, Jim Dine, Paul Georges, Wallace Putnam, Emily Mason and Alice Trumball Mason.

Artists represented by sculpture and for assemblages were: David Smith, Herbert Ferber, Louise Nevelson, Sidney Gordin, Richard Stankiewicz, Varujan Boghosian, William King, Rosati, Sidney Geist, Gross, Zogbaum, Ann Arnold, Fritz Bultman, Stan Freborg, Jackie Ferrara, Tal Streeter, Herbert Kallem, Claes Oldenburg (wooden wall hangings) and John Chamberlain.

The Tirca-Karlis Gallery — Circa 1963

Tirca-Karlis Gallery and Others

On the Bay side of Commercial Street at the foot of Center Street and diagonally across from the Chrysler Museum, a gabled white frame building became, in 1958, the home of one of the town's most distinguished art galleries, called the Tirca-Karlis. The proprietor was a small-framed brown-eyed woman; until a heart murmur developed, Tirca Cohen had followed a career as a dancer and teacher of modern dance. Born in Russia early in this century, she had studied modern dance in Dresden and immigrated to the U.S. in 1950. Teaching modern dance at the Galerie Secession, she met Mark Rothko, Adolph Gottlieb and other American artists whose work appealed to her. She began to buy their paintings and assembled an impressive collection; generously represented was the work of another friend, Milton Avery.

In 1959 she bought the building on Commercial Street and launched into a new career as a dealer. Her opening one-man show was for George Grosz, another emigré from Nazism. The range of her taste was well-defined but not limited to abstraction: she showed Raphael Soyer as well as Robert Motherwell, landscapes by Richard Diebenkorn along with futurist abstractions by Edward Giobbi. In her gallery the drawings of Jules Pascin and Phillip Evergood seemed at home with the abstractions of Budd Hopkins and the lyrically abstract collages of Henry Botkin.

During a protracted battle with cancer she continued to preside over the gallery during the summer of 1974; she died in New York in November of that year. Since then, the Provincetown gallery has been carried on by Karlis Cohen, her husband, who for years had shared responsibility for the enterprise. Among other artists of the gallery were: Nassos Daphnis, George Constant, Joseph Kaplan, Ann Brigadier, the late Alvin Ross, Marcia Marcus, Leo Manso, Lester Johnson and, from Wellfleet, Nora Spayer and Sideo Fromboluti, since 1970, Benny Andrews.

Situated at the bend that Commercial Street makes as it approaches the extreme West End, the *Kessler Gallery* was opened in 1958 by a college teacher from New York, Paul Kessler. An outstanding triumph in his search for vital new talents was the one-man show given in 1960 to Benny Andrews whose soaring reputation took off from that debut. Other early additions — all representational but with a fresh way of seeing and composing — were Sally Michel, March Avery and Violet Sigismund. Work by Paul Pollaro was exhibited in 1965. Among recent exhibitors is Nicholas Sperakis of New York.

In the early 1960's Esther Stuttman ran a gallery by that name in a small midtown space. She showed younger artists whose reputations were in the making, including (in 1962) Warren Brandt.

The *East End Gallery,* situated a block or two east of the HCE on the same harbor side of Commercial, was operated for a number of summers in the early and mid-1960's by Clinton Seely and his partner Donald Jasinsky. In an elongated space they presented such outstanding young artists as John Grillo (one man show in 1963) and Robert Beauchamp, as well as artists of established reputation such as Remo Farruggio, Martin Friedman and Gerrit Hondius.

In 1963 Virginia Zabriskie opened the *Zabriski Gallery* in a converted barn between Mechanic and Cottage Streets which had served successively as a studio for Jackson Pollock, Hans Hofmann and Franz Kline. She showed such artists as Emilio Cruz, Robert DeNiro, Lucas Samaris, Robert Beauchamp, Lester Johnson, Bob Thompson, Nell Blaine and Jan Müller, as well as the work of B. J. O. Nordfeldt, George C. Ault and Abraham Walkowitz.

The tradition of the non-profit cooperative gallery was carried on in the past decade by the *Provincetown Group Gallery* comprised of some of the colony's best known and longest established artists. Situated for many years in a

Chrysler Art Museum, Provincetown — Circa 1965. Left to right: Lila Katzen, Lena Gurr, Walter P. Chrysler, Jr., Ed Giobbi, Helen Frankenthaler, Helen Sawyer, Ross Moffett, Karl Knaths, Morris Davidson, Lily Harmon, Courtney Allen, Sol Wilson, Gerrit Hondius, S. Edmund Oppenheim, Wallace Baseford, Jack Tworkov, Fred Tasch, Bruce McKain, Nassos Daphnis, Howard Kanovitz, Leo Manso, Chaim Gross, Seong Moy, Edwin Dickinson, others unidentified.
Photograph by Harvey Lloyd

basement space in the picturesque midtown Mews (just east of the Chrysler Museum), they moved in 1974 into a first floor gallery of the then-vacant museum building (it was then being converted into a center for visual and performing arts); in 1976 they were established in another space on midtown Commercial Street approaching the East End.

Presented at the *Group Gallery* were the realist landscapes of Hawthorne-trained Bruce McKain; the sweeping, rhythmically textured abstractions of Romanos Rizk, since 1949 a year round resident and teacher; the impressionist figures, landscapes and interiors of S. Edmund Oppenheim, a teacher of long standing at the Art Students League; and the cubistically styled oils, caseins, woodcuts, serigraphs and drawings of long-time summer resident Lena Gurr, who studied with John Sloan and Maurice Sterne. An intoxication with vast perspectives and sweeping skies is seen in the oils and graphics of Richard Florsheim. A strong graphic sense also marks the genre subjects of Association activist, Mervin Jules. Collage is handled with terse simplifications by Connie Black, with adroit spatial dynamics by Marit Jensen (she also paints luminous interiors and landscapes), and with a combination of image and abstraction by Ray Wells. Best known for his brooding clowns, the late Gerrit Hondius also made colors sing in his still life paintings. The figure is elusively present in the luminous watercolor washes of Betty Bodian. In his earlier decorative abstractions (prints and paintings), as well as in his recent works with enigmatic use of images, Seong Moy combines subtle rhythms of his native China with the planar structures of modern art. A point of departure may be a surface composed of old maps or shapes stenciled from factory templates in the abstracted paintings of Katherine Burnside. *The New Yorker's* celebrated cartoonist, Mischa Richter, joined the Group to reveal an alter ego as a painter: light-hearted, close-up vignettes of the Cape scene are shaped with a fluid brush into fresh patterns and off-beat colors.

The Boom Years

Does an artists colony need an art museum? Perhaps not — at least a good case can be made for the summer interlude as a time of digesting the stimulation offered by the big city centers in the winter. But it remains an academic question — what other artists' colony could ever boast a collection of works spanning the history of art from Egyptian and Pre-Columbian down to Pop Art? And all this a stone's throw from the sparkling Bay in a monumental 1850's building, the former Methodist Church (painted by Hopper, Demuth and others) that is itself a work of art! For many the charm of the Chrysler Art Museum, founded in 1958 by the collector and son of the automobile company founder, Walter P. Chrysler, was not in its comprehensiveness but in the chance it provided to discover in an informal setting, works one might not ordinarily seek out: a small gem of a Heronymus Bosch, specimens of Italian and French Baroque not always stylish in the museums at the time, above all a profusion of French, Dutch, Flemish and English nineteenth century masters (some by less familiar artists. For example, a monumental work, *The Neophyte,* by Gustave Dore, known to most people today only through his illustrations for the Bible and Dante's *Inferno*). In addition the Chrysler Museum offered prime examples of Art Nouveau furniture, porcelain and silver, American paintings and sculpture, and, in a separate building, a collection of Sandwich and other art glass, American and French, unsurpassed anywhere in the United States.

Periodically the Museum turned its attention to the town's founding artists (the Hawthorne restrospective of 1961); even contemporaries like Peter Busa, Mischa Richter and Lena Gurr were honored with surveys of their work. And the

An Indian Indian Summer, Chrysler Art Museum — September, 1966. Left to right:
Yeffe Kimball, Medicine Man, Chief Jeffers, Grand Sachem of all the Indians of
Massachusetts, Walter P. Chrysler, Jr., and Ronald A. Kuchta.

90

museum generously collected works of the many well-known and lesser-known artists of Provincetown.

Although the museum was open year-round, each summer offered changing exhibitions, "From Bassano to Van Gogh," and "Provincetown Past & Present" in 1958; "The Controversial Century: 1850–1950," in 1962; "64 Masterpieces from the Chrysler Collection" in 1963; "A Museum's Perspective on Collecting," in 1964; "New Eyes" and "The Twentieth Century, Prototype and Antecedents" in 1965.

The museum's own eclectic collections were steadily expanding with Walter P. Chrysler, Jr., acquiring and giving the museum literally truck loads of art each year. The museum's landscaped lawn and terraces provided a showcase for current attractions that could be very provocative (for instance, Alberto Collie's electronic antipolar floating sculpture; Kusama's body-painting demonstration; Yeffe Kimball's colorful outdoor-cylinder painting, called "Space Continuum;" "An American Indian Summer Festival" with Wampanoag Chiefs in attendance and a barbecue of venison and reindeer meat to celebrate a Native American exhibition). During a two-week engagement of Andy Warhol's *Exploding Plastic Inevitable* (sight and sound ensemble in 1966), interior galleries were transformed by multiple screen projections, and mobile color patterns of light continuously sweeping the walls to the accompaniment of a formidable torrent of acid rock by the Velvet Underground. Experimental art films were also a regular feature at the Museum on summer nights.

In another, less flamboyant, aspect of its services, there was the art library maintained in the basement with admirable efficiency by Mrs. Chrysler; its several thousand volumes spanning the history of art and supplemented by folders and clipping files on contemporaries, was a boon to students, scholars and working art journalists. From 1962 until 1968, Ronald A. Kuchta, presently Director of Everson Museum of Art in Syracuse, New York, was curator of the Museum and a native Provincetowner, Nancy O. Merrill, presently Director of the Sandwich Glass Museum in Sandwich, Massachusetts was curator of glass from 1965 until after the museum moved in 1971.

When the museum opened its doors in July 1958, scores of townsmen and their wives were invited to a gala inaugural banquet together with New York critics and celebrities. But the welcome and good will then lavishly pledged was gradually dissipated. Tensions developed betweeen Walter P. Chrysler, Jr., and the Art Association and also with the selectmen who governed the town. A continuous bone of contention was the need for parking space to accommodate the many museum visitors; this could be obtained only through extensions that were opposed by the town. When Chrysler was adamantly turned down in his demand for an alternate site for the museum, he finally, in 1971, accepted an offer from the city of Norfolk, Virginia (Mrs. Chrysler's hometown), and moved the Chrysler Museum to the South where it is presently located and called the Chrysler Museum at Norfolk. A number of summer residents (led by Rozlyn Garfield, a real-estate agent) made a valiant effort to "save the museum," their regrets over loss of the art works (a reported sixty-million-dollar collection) were compounded by a fear that the beautiful old building would be turned into some sort of neon-lit temple of tourist novelties. (After eight years of varied unsuccessful experiments the building was finally rescued, given landmark status, and, largely through the efforts of Josephine Del Deo, became the home of the Provincetown Heritage Museum. Its displays presently celebrate and record the general history and development of the town in a promising collection of paintings and also document the seven decades of the artists colony.)

The Chrysler Museum brought critics and collectors to Provincetown, and in its first summer took the initiative in staging (in 1958) the Provincetown Arts Festival, a major national open competitive exhibition, assembling the work of nearly 400 artists in enormous white tents erected on grounds above Bradford

Street near the High School. The flags of the states flying above the tents signified that the paintings had been gathered from across the nation (selected by regional juries and collected from eight regional stations). A purchase prize was won by John Ferren, and others went to Semyon Shimin, Milton Goldring and Donald Stoltenberg; cash awards went to David Porter, Hilaire Hiler, Eleanor A. Clark, Will Barnet, Gerald McLaughlin and William Kienbusch.

Not all the cultural attractions in Provincetown were competitive. Each summer there were two symphony concerts with an orchestra conducted by Jo Hawthorne, son of Charles W. Hawthorne (he is now conductor of the Duluth Symphony Orchestra). On a midtown wharf there was live theater by the Provincetown Playhouse directed by the venerable actess, Catherine Huntington, offering a repertory of plays ranging from O'Neill and Colette to even more contemporary dramas.

In 1964 the Provincetown Art Association celebrated its Golden Anniversary with an exhibition of nearly 200 paintings plus a selection of prints, drawings and sculpture representing the colony's artists by early and late examples. For those less acquainted with the work of early residents it was interesting to see John Noble's moody *Sardine Fishermen* of 1920 and, from the same year, Nancy Ferguson's lively *Friends Meet Friends,* and from 1928, *Potato Planters* by Ross Moffett. In the 1960's the Association was constantly expanding its special programs: it offered series of jazz concerts, discussions, poetry readings, technical demonstrations, lectures and dance performances.

In 1963 when Ivan Karp had opened O. K. Harris, the town's first and only gallery devoted entirely to Pop Art, the Art Association held a symposium on *Pop Art* with Karp the leading spokesman for the affirmative position, with theoretical support for the movement from Witgenstein. Critical of the then radically new style, in an evening continuously sparked by jibes, laughter and stunts (Budd Hopkins brought a papier maché ax), were poet Stanley Kunitz and Hopkins, with Dorothy Seckler on the fence.

To Karp's assertion that "(Pop Art is) the American acclamation of the unseemly beauty of the American spectacle . . . a kind of joyousness at the beauty of the ungainly spectacle . . . ," Kunitz identified Pop with "the movement of anti-art in the century . . . one of the most important tides of art history. Ever since Duchamp painted the moustache on the Mona Lisa . . . there has been along with this movement a rejection of the naturally poetic or beautiful or lyrical." Kunitz said there was nothing especially fallacious in seeking beauty in the most sordid aspects of contemporary experience, but "the great tradition of art requires some transformation, some metamorphosis in the making of an art form." Later Kunitz read an 1883 letter from Vincent Van Gogh describing his excitement on having discovered a great garbage pile at the Hague: "These things that people threw away . . . virtually a paradise for the artist." Said Kunitz: "Of course he did see the garbage, he saw the possibilities there too, but he saw it in relation to the whole framework of human experience."

Witgenstein, always caustically witty, said that art has no morality: "Manet's *Olympia* was considered pornographic in 1863. Today she looks like a harmless bag lying on a couch waiting for a bus to Westchester." Budd Hopkins spoke of the Pop artist's insistence on finding deep meaning in non-art or some inexpressive thing. An example was someone who goes to the movies and dismisses Fellini's *Eight and a Half* as merely sentimental but says: "The Woody Woodpecker was filled with meaning!" The moderator of this evening of timely and crackling exchange was Mervin Jules.

Provincetown has always been able to attract and hold for long periods brilliant, top-flight writers and poets — O'Neill, Dos Passos and e. e. cummings (both of the latter also painters), to mention only a few. In the last two decades when some celebrities were taking flight from this "tourist trap," Provincetown remained a home and favorite place for two of America's greatest literary men: Stanley Kunitz, the national laureate, living for half the year in the East End, and Norman Mailer sending off his barrages of literary fireworks from the other end of town.

As a close friend of Rothko, Kline, Hofmann and other leading members of the New York School, Kunitz can hardly avoid being drawn into forums and causes. He is sought out as a spokesman for the liberal humanist point of view. Hoping to spend most of his non-writing time cultivating his superb garden he nevertheless played a major role in launching and sustaining the writers' program of the Provincetown Fine Arts Work Center.

Mailer is seen here and there but seldom formally. In the 1960's he produced his play *The Deer Park* in the basement of a small hotel, and he was himself sometimes on the scene. With his roving life — overseas to make a film, back and forth to Washington prodding the conscience of the political establishment — he still finds time to touch base at his home in Provincetown.

Among other literati on the Cape End year-round are poet Mary Oliver (in Provincetown) and Alan Dugan (in Truro). Art authority and novelist, B. H. Friedman, a pillar of FAWC, summers on the Cape End.

Among the schools that attracted students each summer to Provincetown, the largest was probably the *Provincetown Workshop School* on Commercial Street not far from the Art Association. Founded by Victor Candell and Leo Manso, painters long established in the community, the school opened its doors in 1958 offering a free-wheeling program that allowed a great deal of individual choice within a framework of modern disciplines to students who were no longer beginners. Through its generous scholarship program the school attracted students from many parts of the country, especially the South.

Launched in 1944 in the same location atop Miller Hill that had served first the Hawthorne and then the Hofmann Schools, the Morris Davidson School of Contemporary Painting also offers composition in an abstract idiom but with an emphasis on the potential for psychological expression for each individual.

Hawthorne's impressionistically optical approach to painting still inspires the method taught at Henry Hensche's Cape School at 48 Pearl Street. It may be the only school that still sends students with their painting gear out to the dunes, lanes and beaches to squint in the sunlight or fog in order to measure and transpose the scale of color tones in the scene before them. After more than 45 years, during which he has continued as a productive painter, Hensche can claim a devoted body of alumni, including Franz Kline and Edward Giobbi who always acknowledged Hensche as their master.

At 7 Brewster Street the well-known painter and printmaker for more than two decades, Seong Moy, taught courses in etching, woodcut and lithography as well as classes in painting and drawing with a modern approach.

Milton Avery: The Cape via Zen 1956–1959

Milton Avery (1893–1965) produced his climactic works on the theme of sea and shore from an apartment over the waterfront not far from the hectic bustle of midtown. For the first time, in the later 1950's, he was working on large canvases, but the grander scale was not the only reason the old marine subjects looked so stunningly new in these paintings. As in the work of children and in many of the masterpieces of oriental scroll painting, the vantage point of the artist seemed to be everywhere and nowhere. Avery did not say that it was through his studies of Zen, extending over decades (Mark Rothko had been impressed by the Zen poetry in Avery's studio during the mid-1930's when he was an Avery disciple), that the duality of subject and object had been transcended, but he did tell his wife, Sally, that every picture was completely visualized in his head before he

The Harbor from Delst Haven, West End

picked up a brush. In paintings like *Tangerine Moon, Wine Dark Sea* and *Dunes and Sea,* Avery created a kind of pictorial space as immediate as anything achieved by the Abstract Expressionists, and this immediacy was all the more compelling because it was conveyed with serenity and detachment.

In Provincetown as in New York he preferred to paint in the family living quarters, part of the flow of intimate life around him. Never in any point in his career had Avery worked in a separate studio equipped with a skylight or other assumed requisites. Instead of a distraction, the movements of his wife, Sally Michel, at her daily routines supplied a reassuring rhythm. His quick sketches of Sally, his daughter, March, or occasional visitors in unposed attitudes were the basis of his figure paintings. He never used a model.

Some of his best work was done in the second story space of the Peter Hunt house (leased from the well known artist-decorator); it offered a fine view of the Bay. Another advantage that he had never before enjoyed was that large canvases could be hauled up by ropes from the Studio Shop next door. Reflecting on one of these monumental seascapes, Milton Avery wrote in October 1959: "It was my third summer in Provincetown. Weeks of wet weather had discouraged me. Then a day cleared, but the atmosphere was still oppressive. That evening I sat on my deck facing Provincetown Bay. The water was moody — wine dark. Across the bay the lights of Wellfleet were a row of buttons on the horizon. Suddenly above the lights appeared a surprising moon, tangerine in color and shape. It made magic. A week later I painted 'Tangerine Moon' and 'Wine Dark Sea.'"

The new large canvases were painted almost as quickly as the modest sized ones of previous years. He worked with intense concentration without changes or retouching (in this he was like the Japanese masters of the Sumi style). He could finish a sizeable picture in a morning. Before brush was touched to canvas he had assimilated the essentials in a state of mind that has been described as a kind of meditative dreaming. In his "mind's eye," a scheme of space-creating color planes was already fitted together. Usually he would begin painting at the bottom of the canvas — often a land mass or shore — and wind up later with the sky that could be any color, even yellow or pink, that completed the lambent whole.

Avery's flatly luminous color shapes and surprising juxtapositions had been called Matisse-like since the 1940's. But his Provincetown landscapes, with their extended fields of color-patterns and colors made to "breathe" through dry-brush texturing, elicited a new recognition of the "plasticity" of his color. Hans Hofmann said that Avery was the first American to understand color as a creative means.

Wolf Kahn accompanied him once on a sketching jaunt to Corn Hill. More often Avery found a subject close to his studio: a favorite one was the "flats," especially interesting in this part of the harbor shore at low tide. There was a gentle humour in his drawings and paintings of the shore birds gathered there in sprightly colonies at sundown. After a decade in which painters attracted to landscape had been made to feel that working from motifs of sea and shore could be productive of nothing but "corn," Avery was opening a fresh approach to the loved and familiar scene.

After a heart attack in the late 1950's, it was necessary for Avery to be closer to his doctor and to New York City. He spent the remaining summers of his life in a quiet spot in the wooded hills outside Woodstock, New York. At the memorial service following his death of heart disease in 1965, Mark Rothko said: "He was first of all a poet ... This took great courage in a generation that felt it could only be heard through clamour, force and show of power — His gentleness proved more audible and poignant."

Peter Hutchinson with dog at his home on Holway Avenue, 1976

Nature in Image and Symbol

Aside from the work of Milton Avery and only partially in response to his example, a rediscovery of the Cape End scene was in progress in the late 1950's and early 1960's, at a time when the landscape itself was increasingly viewed through the interstices of commercial structures. Yet the early-morning departures and evening returns of the fishing fleet still set a rhythm for the life of the harborfront through golden summer days.

Probably this renewed interest in the nature theme was a response less to the exterior world than to fresh possibilities opened up through the resources of painting itself.

Because of the simplified shapes and lambent colors of his coastal scenes, perhaps also because of a similarly gentle temperament, *Herman Maril* (1908–   ) has been linked by some critics to Avery but, the airy, open expanses of his shore subjects are differently structured. Maril employs spare linear elements both to characterize forms and to suggest a framework in which he suspends softly ragged shapes over quiet seas.

With thin oil washes softly textured in juxtaposed vignettes, *Tony Vevers* (1926–   ) often painted on a single canvas a sequence of scenes from the life around him: a softly contoured figure, a path, evening skies, objects. Perhaps this format served as another way of bridging the gap between the perceiver and what was perceived. Later in a parallel venture, he created banded abstractions from earth and sand affixed to canvas.

Sally Michel handled landscape with a more directly sensuous touch, but, like her husband Milton Avery, she visualized a subject in flattened shapes. Her daughter, *March Avery,* often chose the intimate vignette as her motif and transposed it into soft patterns and off-beat colors with poetry and understated wit.

The light and colors of nature were inventively transposed into abstract images with strong associative appeal by the late Sidney Gross whose fantasy led him in one series to suggest the experience of space exploration. *Remo Farruggio* (1906–   ), a colonist known for the distinctive color of his abstract paintings, over a long summer residency, creates an air of mystery with lights aglow in softly diffused planes. With a background in traditional painting, *Romanos Rizk* (1927–   ), who heads his own school, has recently focused on expressing energies and rhythms in nature in monumental canvases swept with painterly textures in diagonal movements.

There was a Rococo elegance in the sensuous and lyrical chromatic schemes of *Angelo Ippolito* (1922–   ), who had been an advanced student in the Hofmann classes. His work was subsequently featured at the Sun and HCE galleries. A pulsation of movement across the canvas was maintained through the sweep of a loaded brush.

Wolf Kahn (1927–   ) whose hair's breadth escape from Nazi Germany brought him to the U.S. in adolescence, turned away from his early love of landscape during years of study with Hofmann when he pursued an elusive abstract perfection. When nature subjects were restored to his work it was initially through a flux of color strokes. Later with a softly plied brush and reliance on his superb eye for tones plus a magic with tremulous edges, he developed a style that transmits the "breathing" quality of field and forest and the noble endurance of weathered buildings.

Provincetown's best known Conceptual artist, a summer resident of many years, is *Peter Hutchinson* (1930–   ); his witty and perceptive writing on emerging directions have gained him a new reputation in art publications. Hutchinson's responses to nature were apt to be documented in photographs, written comments and sometimes in a sequence of small graphic variations like his *Alphabet* series.

In *Martin Friedman* (1896–   ), Provincetown has its Redon; no corporeal humans walk his misty horizons or are guided by the glow of soft wandering satellites in a violet gloom. From his picturesquely situated studio and home off Bradford Street in the East End, *Irving Marantz* (1912–1973) painted frieze-like figures in simplified settings; a slow rhythm and resonant color accentuated a muralesque quality. After he turned to acrylics late in his career he produced figures and still life in a series of small pictures notable for their spontaneity and light touch.

Bryon Browne (1907–1961) approached nature through inventive linear structures. A respected name in the ranks of abstract artists since the 1930's, Browne was also a romantic in temperament; in one instance a fiery sunset image was planted among his intricate Cubist planes. A year-round resident of Provincetown for many years, *Joe Kaplan* (1900–   ) composes landscapes in oil with a rare painterly finesse and a sure ordering of luminous spaces. He has observed every detail and nuance of a scene, then given pure sensibility and mood the upper hand. With a brush and black ink he works in a more oriental vein. Like the Japanese Sumi artist, he allows the white of the paper to sing, and can evoke a forest or a wave with a swift accent or a spatter. A gifted young artist, the late *Gandy Brodie* (1924–1975) developed a spirited personal style of expressionist-realism. With juicy paint he could extract a memorable image from the ordinarily banal subject of a seagull on a piling, or a milk container on a table.

As a very young girl, *Marjorie Windust* (Mrs. Nathan Halper) studied with Hawthorne in Provincetown. From her harbor-side house in the East End (formerly her family's summer home) she occasionally painted the sea in airy bands of tone, but more often is absorbed in an elusive and subjective art of fluid, dancing shapes in subtle colors.

Nora Speyer and *Sideo Fromboluti* (1920–   ) usually work from a close-up perception of nature motifs they find in the woods, streams and garden of their lakeside home in Wellfleet. Fiery flowers projecting a mysterious intensity turn up in Speyer's canvases. In a well known series Fromboluti orchestrated subtle variations of green-golds in a richly encrusted triptych on the theme of lily pads. Another artist working with thick impastos was the late *Nanno de Groot* whose unusually designed home and studio, marked by twin high-pitched roofs, is a landmark in the East End. Through the rhythmic plying of a loaded brush, De Groot (1913–1963) seemed at times to be remembering his countryman, Vincent Van Gogh, but the color of his sailboats and flowers could be simplified to a dominance of whites. In a quiet mood and with pleasant directness, *Violet Sigismund* painted a harborfront scene as a comfortable ambience for her deck rocking chair and other intimate objects. *Roslyn Roose* painted the Cape landscape in a semi-abstract manner with color a major emphasis. Cubist planes become a decorative framework in the intimate landscape paintings and prints of *Lena Gurr* (1897–   ), a former student of Maurice Sterne who is an activist in the Art Association of many years standing.

Richard Florsheim's (1916–   ) paintings and graphic work are the subject of a recent book by Dean August L. Freundlich of Syracuse University. From his waterfront studio and home in the East End Florsheim produces paintings and lithographs of vast cloud-swept skies seen through rhythmic lattices of vertical masts, a linear equivalent in Provincetown of the lake-front industrial structures multiplied by reflections, that fascinate him in his native Chicago. Largely self-taught, Florsheim approaches his work in the light of a broad humanist philosophy. He is an officer of the Art Association and on the board of the Fine Arts Work Center. Graphic work as well as paintings shaped by social convictions were important in bringing early recognition in the career of *Mervin Jules* who is also a well known university teacher. In contrast to his former satirical realism, the focus of his recent paintings and graphics on motifs in his intimate surroundings, has been poetic and personal.

98

Arthur Cohen (1928–   ) who had not painted until he was 30 decided to move from commercial drawings to serious work as a realist painter as the result of a brief contact with Edwin Dickinson who served as a substitute teacher at Cooper Union in 1948. Cohen was fascinated by Dickinson's precision and by his eccentricities. Decades later he came to Provincetown and launched into a series of paintings filled with expanses of sky and bay, a sliver of luminous land dividing them. He disagreed with the label of "magic realist" applied by critics generally in approbation of a novel treatment of a familiar theme. He paints from direct observation, often from his car or from the De Groot house.

Living in a waterfront studio near Fisherman's Wharf in the early 1960's, *Peter Dechar* (1942–   ) was just beginning to attract favorable attention from critics who compared the mysterious images he composed of giant pears, to the painted enigmas of René Magritte. Occupying most of the canvas, his subtle, painted pears — brooding presences alone or in monumental groups — were partially enveloped by shadows seeming to stretch to faraway horizons.

A few doors away on the waterfront, *Alvin Ross* (1920–1975) was creating his own magic with modest-sized paintings of very small things. With its jewel-like surface and meticulous detail, a Ross picture of berries in a basket could pass for an old master. A popular lecturer on art history at Pratt Institute and New York University, Ross had been influenced by Renoir and Matisse in an early stage of his career, and explored a variant of surrealism before developing a style for which "magic realist" seemed only an approximate tag. One summer when he was in love with whites he painted, against expanses of white tablecloth, a group of egg shells and eggs. Bakery products inspired another unexpectedly haunting series: a marble cake with a wedge lifted out said as much about light as many a beach scene.

For *Sharli Powers Land,* a former fellow and officer of the Fine Arts Work Center, whose work has also been seen at the Art Association, the creation of an authentic Cape subject seems to be a matter of a fine perception of light, painterly elan, and a completely open mind about the pictorial priorities. She has painted garages and street traffic across the way from her studio, and she can say a lot about nature in pictures of the growing things inside and outside her window.

Lily Harmon (1912–   ), an influential colonist, long established in her studio and home in the East End, is as skilled and sensitive in handling the harbor landscape as in her drawings and paintings of the figure.

Salvadore Del Deo, one of the colony's best-known and most civic-minded personalities, is a painter, teacher and distinguished restaurateur. Sal's Place in the East End is a summer gathering place for artists, writers and gourmets. The feeling for light he developed in studies with Hensche is still evident in his work, but by the 1950's he had become sufficiently adventurous in his style to be invited into the innovating group at the Sun Gallery. In some of his landscapes bright sunshine is replaced by nuanced tones in an airy but deftly ordered space, with soft touches of the brush insuring an all-over flow of movement. Heightened color and sweeping shadows accentuate mood and mystery in recent figure compositions. In the winter Del Deo teaches a children's art class for a charge of twenty-five cents a lesson.

In the work of *Yeffee Kimball* (1914–   ), the colony's colorful artist of part Osage Indian ancestry, reference to nature can be symbolic or abstract. She returns at times to the mysterious animal images seen in her early work — in this vein a buffalo may be a luminous white shape on a night-like ground. In the late 1950's in a series she called "cosmic," she used lucite to effect a bubbling flow and intermingling of colors. An author of books and articles on Indian lore, she enjoys a leadership role in the conduct of Indian affairs nationally.

S. Edmund Oppenheim, well-known portraitist and respected teacher at the Art Students League, has been an established figure in the colony for decades. Appealingly reminiscent of the old ways is his popular painting of an artist setting out toward the dunes under open summer skies with his gear strapped to his back. Oppenheim's attention to telling detail in the stance and gesture of his subjects bespeaks an admiration for Degas but his preference for a softly diffused light would link him to other Impressionists.

Mischa Richter whose cartoons appear regularly in the *New Yorker* doubles as a painter with an eye attuned to chromatic interplay. His Cape End scenes are subtly schematic, composed with a delight in shapes turning into patterns even as they denote parasols, tables, parts of a wharf, rippling water. His brush is spontaneous but controlled, permitting no loose ends.

Discontinuities — With Scissors and Paste

Increasingly a feature at the prestigious galleries by the early 1960's were works created with scissors and paste: collage alone or combined with painting. Although collage was city-bred and could be seen as an expression of a sense of discontinuity anywhere, it seemed overnight to have gained acceptance in Provincetown and to flourish on every level from amateur to avant-garde. With the powerful exception of Benny Andrews, it is fair to say that by the time collage reached Provincetown it had lost its Dadaist bite; it no longer implied either an anti-art stance nor did it become a vehicle for ironic jabs at the Cape environment. Collage encouraged a sense of play with materials and offered a chance to concentrate on formal elements without the distraction of representation.

Whether from New York or the Cape, the example of *Robert Motherwell* was influential. He was now living in the East End and his collages combined with painting were seen at the Art Association as well as at the HCE and Tirca-Karlis galleries. Motherwell talked about his collages at Smith College: "About collage. For example, the labels in my collages from 'Gauloises,' 'players,' I sometimes smoke them ... The papers in my collages are usually things that are familiar to me, part of my life ... Collages are a modern substitute for still-life ... Traditional still-life seems funny in America, but in Europe completely natural since you see one at the end of each meal. In collage there are a lot of ready-made details, for when one wants details. My painting deals in large simplifications for the most part. Collage in contrast is a way to work with autobiographical material — which one wants sometimes ... I do feel more joyful with collage, less austere. A form of play. Which painting, in general, is not, for me at least ... "

Fritz Bultman (1919–   ) finds collage a medium in which he can generate ideas that are later continued in paintings and also in the three dimensions of sculpture. His shaping with scissors parallels working from an armature with clay in that he can compose from the center outward and is less confined by the need to relate to a frame. Large sheets of heavy paper — to be cut in flaring shapes — are painted in saturated oranges and blues, dark browns, and blacks, and often set off from each other by bordering strips, paint over the binding edge of spiral notebooks. The attractively rough and ready look is not lost even when the ensemble is mounted on expanses of linen. The rhythm of the ensemble is boldly dynamic.

For *Budd Hopkins* (1931–   ) collage is more than a handy technique — it is a state of mind. In composing with jarring elements and disparate styles he expresses a philosophic viewpoint in which discontinuities are recognized as a vital aspect of contemporary life. His large geometric abstractions have their beginnings in small collages composed of painted fragments that retain the artist's spontaneous touch. But scale has its importance too where the maximum

Motherwell & Frankenthaler's studio

contrast of opposite means is intended. In some recent works where separate painterly panels are fastened onto geometric units, the result is assemblage. Even before coming to Provincetown in the middle 1950's, Hopkins had been influenced by Motherwell who had lectured at Oberlin when Hopkins was a student there. Living in Wellfleet with his wife, April Kingsley, a writer and critic, Hopkins remains active in the colony as a lecturer as well as a painter.

Anne Brigadier (1908–   ), a Cape resident since 1930, moved to Provincetown in the 1940's and later became the first woman trustee of the Art Association. She is the author of a book on collage published by Watson-Guptill in which she explains the preparation of materials for collage from oil in water prints, monoprints, rubbings, laminated tissues and granular materials, most of which she has used in her own work. Encaustic is also important in her collage method, which is aimed at poetic evocation through delicately textured fields.

Very influential in exploring collage and demonstrating the enlargement of its possibilities, has been *Leo Manso* (1914–   ), a resident since 1947 and, until its closing in 1976, co-director with Victor Candell, of the Provincetown Workshop school. Manso has been deeply affected by studies in Eastern thought which he pursues on travels in India, Nepal and elsewhere in the orient. He sometimes evokes the rhythms and impersonal symbolic presence of Tantric art in collages of aged papers, rags, scorched and stained fabrics and even more mysteriously textured materials. In the 29 collages of his recent series, *The Valley of Kathmandu,* exquisite fragments were combined as organic, spatially suggestive layers within the tondo shape. In the early 1960's he composed with a soft geometry, contrasting symmetrical with asymmetrical shapes.

Henry Botkin (1896–   ) finds collage "a technique that sparks the mind and expands ideas." Associated for many years with his cousin, George Gershwin, and the circle around the composer, Botkin gave up a lucrative career in commercial art to devote himself to painting, initially in a traditional vein. By the early 1950's when he was a founding member of the cooperative Gallery 256, he had turned to abstraction, and by the end of that decade collage combined with painting was absorbing him completely. Aiming, he says, at "poetic transformation," Botkin composes irregularly-shaped fabric cutouts so that they move mysteriously in and out of the painterly field of a canvas. The airy encounter of arcs, diamonds and handle-like strips can be sportive or grave. Botkin's collages, varied in size and mood, were seen almost annually in one man shows at the Tirca-Karlis Gallery.

In 1960 *Benny Andrews* (1930–   ) spent his last money on a ticket for the bus from New York to Provincetown; the occasion was the opening at the Paul Kessler Gallery of his first one-man show of paintings, including some with collage elements. Two years later he had developed a following in Provincetown. In a relaxed way, different from New York, he met a number of well-known artists. Chaim Gross brought people to see his work, among them, Bella Fishko, who asked him to join her new Forum Gallery in New York. Andrews said that when he arrived in Provincetown the place looked like heaven: "When I got out on the Cape it was like another world ... the grass, the sand, water and all that looked surreal." At first, because it was so expensive, he could stay for only a couple of weeks. Later when his pictures were selling in the city, he could have stayed but he felt the art climate had changed. "Less and less serious-minded people came to Provincetown each summer," he wrote, and he described "people who do (no) more than gawk or eat French fries and drink Coke while wandering through one's show."

In one-man shows each summer at the Kessler Gallery during the sixties, and after that at the Tirca-Karlis Gallery, Andrews demonstrated a different role for collage—as an accessory to a powerful realism. There is an electric exchange between the painted figure and the applied material: the emotional reality of the image is held in tension with the palpable reality of the thing.

In an opposite vein of emotion directed toward the precise ordering of forms, were the collages of *Edward Giobbi* (1906–   ); they were always among the most provocative works exhibited each year (in one-man shows) at the Tirca-Karlis Gallery. The materials were intentionally simple: corrugated cardboard glued to wood with pastel color added in brusque accents. The effect was dynamic and unexpectedly elegant, the collage elements a foil for the surface agitation of repeated patterns. Through cutouts and juxtaposed, recessed panels, Giobbi obtained a spatial and kinetic play in line with his Futurist aesthetic.

Industrial plastics and factory templates have stimulated fresh inventions for *Katherine Burnside,* as have junkyard castoffs for one-time Hawthorne student, *Catherine Cole Smith,* and frayed fabrics for *Renita Johnson. Carl Ashby* has capitalitzed on media contrasts; *Ray Martan Wells* has extracted from scissored drawings and media pages, images that are psychologically provocative and formally stimulating. Art educator, *Judith Langland,* juxtaposes elements from her spatially mysterious ink drawings. Found materials have been exploited for their associative impact by long time colony activist, *Helen Avlon; Rosalie Atkins* has shaped dynamic designs from linens and metallic papers.

Perspectives

By the summers of the mid-1960's, the churning progress of men and machines on the midtown blocks of Commercial Street was a jerky pantomime of frustration. Between snarled cars and reckless bikes, pedestrians pressed forward in a trot, consuming hot dogs and cotton candy, spilling off the sidewalks or backing up to gawk at souvenir-jammed shop windows or the pavement booths offering quick crayon portraits, caricatures and silhouettes. Many supposed these quick-sketch experts to be the famous artists of Provincetown. Meanwhile, the serious artists complained they were unable because of the traffic impasse, to maintain contact with each other in the old easy ways. Parading in the midst of day-tripping families and staid townsmen, individuals in heavy makeup and bizarre costumes seemed to be acting out some private script. Not all the young people with abundant hair and tattered jeans were the rootless "hippies" so often in trouble with the police. Many were hard-working craftsmen whose wares filled the shops; others were art students, dancers and musicians.

In August, 1970 a forum titled "What Is Happening to Our Art Colony" drew to the Art Association a crowd of about 200, mostly artists and including one art critic. It was not the first time the alarming question had been asked; guilt and blame always accompanied it. Critic Katherine Kuh said the fault was with the artists who had let it be known they had discovered a spot of great beauty and charm. Hordes of people always follow the artists, she said, "to enjoy and destroy" the locale. Artist and teacher Victor Candell said that the problem was "probably national, a matter of numbers." Realtor Rozlyn Garfield thought the real trouble was in the real estate boom. "There are only a half dozen studios left," she said, "and they rent for $1500 a season." Several blamed the lack of parking space; collectors were not able to stop and shop at the galleries. John Frank blamed the Art Association because it had resisted change. Catherine Huntington, founder of the Provincetown Playhouse, stated that her theater would continue to lose money until the town could control the enormous number of people. The Selectmen were accused of insensitivity to the lack of tourist interest in purchasing art. Ronald Shuebrook, a fellow at the Fine Arts Work Center, called for an effort "to embrace the new, to embrace the difficult."

Commercial Street

104

Voices outside this forum were already on the record. Hans Hofmann always thought the ruin of Provincetown began when the four-lane highway went through in 1957. John D. Bell, writing for the Art Association's 1973 catalog, pointed to a double bind: "The automobile has changed the town more drastically than any other factor. It is directly responsible for the establishment in 1961, of the Cape Cod National Seashore, without which the sand dunes would long since have been leveled for motels and parking lots. The seashore, in turn, lures more visitors."

Most of the viewers-with-alarm at the 1970 forum were concerned with the blight that had fallen on two summer months of each year. There was always one voice — that of Phil Malicoat — reminding all that "for ten months of the year Provincetown is a fine place to work." And indeed anyone who has stayed a few weeks past Labor Day can only agree. The honky-tonk vanishes, the streets are quiet, almost deserted, beaches are clean, dunes pristine, the harbor reclaimed by the fishing fleet and gleaming sails. In the late 1960's those who dreamed of restoring Provincetown to its pre-tourist character were also beginning to focus on the ten un-touristed months and to visualize a small nucleus of young artists, in the words of Hudson Walker, "bringing new blood into the community, and encouraging artists to settle here." The result was the Fine Arts Work Center founded in 1968 "to give young writers and visual artists the chance to live on their own and work, after completing their technical training."

Since Hudson Walker and his wife, Ione, settled in Provincetown in 1945 in a large house in the East End, they had become patrons and committed participants in the colony. In this, Hudson was hewing to a family tradition of the Walkers, a wealthy Minneapolis family which spent much of the fortune it had made in lumbering on works of art. Hudson Walker, who had been president of the Art Association and president of the American Federation of Arts, was also the first president of the center; he was directly responsible for getting the center on its feet by convincing the American Federation to sponsor the first year of the program, following its initial sponsoring by the Provincetown Art Association. Later (after incorporation in 1971), help came from the Massachusetts Council on the Arts and Humanities and the National Endowment for the Arts.

In 1972 it was possible to purchase a substantial property at 24 Pearl Street and to set up studios and living space for 15 fellows. The fellows themselves constructed an outstanding gallery named in the summer of 1976 for Hudson Walker. It remains open all summer serving the community with quality exhibitions, poetry readings and slide lectures.

The proportion of visual arts fellows to writer fellows varies from year to year. Most receive a modest grant, and all can benefit from contact with established professionals. Among those who have been available for consultation were Fritz Bultman, Myron Stout, Jim Forsberg, Jack Tworkov, Judith Rothschild and Alvin Ross. About one third of the fellows who complete their stay at the Center remain in the community.

The summer colony has its own prospects for renewal among which is a plan for dividing the town into historic districts (probably two zones) in which landmark buildings are located. This project is spearheaded by Josephine Del Deo whose success in establishing the Provincetown Heritage Museum has encouraged both the artists' colony and the community as a whole. The museum will continue to reflect not only the colorful past but also accomplishments of the present.

The Provincetown Art Association is opening an extensive new wing that will provide safe storage and exhibition space for its growing collection and facilitate effective presentation of its annual shows.

The summer of 1977 will see the launching of a new cooperative, the Longpoint Gallery, in the redesigned space a few short blocks east of the Art Association that formerly housed the Provincetown Workshop school. Among the artists exhibiting (one-man shows for members, along with group show features) are the distinguished assemblage artist and long-time summer resident, Varujan Boghosian, sculptor Sidney Simon and painters Rick Klauber, Fritz Bultman, Carmen Cicero, Edward Giobbi, Nora Speyer, Paul Resika, Sidney Fromboluti, Budd Hopkins, Tony Vevers, Leo Manso, Judith Rothschild and Robert Motherwell. There will be room for outsized works, and the cooperative plans panel discussions, film showings and other special events open to the public.

Some of the young craftsmen speak of Provincetown as a "high energy center," meaning that it has a potential for extremes of every kind — beauty and ugliness, good and evil. Certainly turbulence can be expected from almost any gathering; contention is just as likely to seethe in the meetings of the Selectmen as in the councils of the Art Association. It seems unlikely the town will ever settle into the kind of nostalgic mold with museum-like appeal as has, for instance, Nantucket.

Artists grumble and grieve about what has been lost to civilization, staying as far as possible on the periphery of this town that lives so feverishly in the present. The roster of artists in the new Longpoint Gallery is only a partial representation of the distinguished artists who remain faithful to the Cape End. Robert Motherwell told Ronald Kuchta recently that Provincetown is his "favorite of all places."

Dorothy Gees Seckler

NOTES ON OTHER EUROPEAN AND AMERICAN ARTISTS' COLONIES

Barbizon

The first artists' colony in the Western world might easily have been launched in England where Constable and Turner celebrated landscape untrammeled and unidealized with such power and originality. English artists, however, were to conduct their forays into the countryside on an individual basis. But when the impulse toward an art devoted to innocent nature crossed the Channel, it inspired a gifted group of painters to forsake Paris for extended working sojourns at the village of Barbizon on the edge of the forest Fountainebleau. The virtue of this countryside was the unpretentious naturalness of gentle meadows, winding streams and pleasant woodlands — an absolute contrast to the contrived arcadias and artificial gardens approved by the Academy. This shift from an urban to a rural art center began around 1830, a time when Paris was torn by political uprisings (Delacroix painted his *Liberty Leading the People* in 1830).

No classes were conducted at Barbizon nor did the artists adhere to any one style. Most of them venerated the Dutch landscape painters and admired the English romantics but they shared a belief that the task of the artist was to learn from nature itself rather than from art theory.

Although they all made landscape studies on the spot, paintings were generally executed in the studio nearby. Charles Francois Daubigny was the only one to paint landscapes entirely out of doors; anticipating the Impressionists, he even rigged up a studio on a rowboat for first hand observation of river scenes. Nature worship, developed to a religious intensity, prompted Theodore Rousseau to invest with ardent feeling every detail of field and foliage. He settled permanently in the village of Barbizon along with Jean Francois Millet.

In Millet's drawings and paintings of the village peasants at their daily tasks (which he often endowed with the anatomies he admired in the work of Michelangelo), he was giving form to an idea that was to develop generative force in subsequent artists' colonies: the idea first enunciated by Jean Jacques Rousseau more than a century earlier of the purity and freedom of Man in a natural state (uncorrupted by society). His paintings of noble peasants were scorned by French officialdom for decades but Durand-Ruel shipped them across the Atlantic to become (in prints and reproductions) a requisite badge of culture for the American home. At the very time when Americans were most bent on destroying what was pastoral in their landscape they took Millet's rustics to their hearts and perhaps for the very reasons that made Baudelaire "want to hate them." He wrote: "Whether they are reaping or sowing, whether they are grazing or shearing their animals, they always seem to be saying 'We are the poor and disinherited of this earth but it is we who make it fertile.'"

Pont-Aven

The unique identification of locale and idea, with place becoming the very embodiment of a style for a group of artists, was exceptionally clear in Pont-Aven in the late 1880's. The idea was symbolism (synthesism), the place a village of old, slate-roofed houses set in craggy hills near the Aven River, the mood was mystical, medieval, above all, primitive. In numbers barely enough to comprise a colony some generally academically-trained painters came from England,

Scandanavia and America. Their attention came to be riveted on two who arrived in 1888—first Paul Gauguin and then his young friend, Émile Bernard.

Few of them would have been there except for the cheap living; only sixty-five francs a month for board and lodging at the Pension Gloanec where Gauguin had improvised a studio in the attic. But Gauguin left no doubt of the deep impression the place had made on him since he first visited Pont-Aven in 1886. In a letter rejecting Vincent Van Gogh's invitation to join him in the South, Gauguin wrote: "I love Brittany, I find wilderness and primitiveness there." To his friend, Schuffenecker he confided an even more explicit link between the place and what he hoped to paint: "When my wooden shoes ring on this granite, I hear the muffled, dull and powerful tone which I try to achieve in painting." The visual-associative elements were exactly right to nourish the forms then in gestation in his imagination: the austere landscape, superstitiously devout peasants wearing regional costumes, the flaring ritual bonnets worn by church-going women. The intense Catholicism of young Émile Bernard added an intellectual equivalent.

In this period of unrest and doubt following Gauguin's aborted sojourn in Martinique, Bernard's bold and confident experiments with simplified forms supplied the needed catalyst. Here were the flattened, boldly-outlined shapes that had drawn Gauguin to Japanese prints, no longer simply decorative, but fired with mystical belief. Now visually saturated by a mode of life that constantly evoked the mysticism and wild superstition of the medieval world, he saw that such cloisonné-like designs might transcend decoration, become charged with symbolic feeling. In his turning-point painting, *Jacob Wrestling with the Angel,* he brought into stunning synthesis all the elements—aesthetic, primitive, symbolic—that in Pont-Aven had answered to his own fevered search for some meaning not to be found in the world of commerce and materialism.

Woodstock, New York

Neither John Ruskin nor William Morris ever visited the Catskills but the founding of an artists' colony in Woodstock, New York, in 1902 was a direct result of the impact of their ideals on two exceptional men. Ralph Radcliffe Whitehead, a wealthy English idealist and man of letters, had studied with Ruskin at Oxford's Bailliol College in 1880; ever since he had dreamed of founding an ideal commune. It was to provide the kind of sympathetic conditions for creative work formulated by Ruskin and at the same time fulfill Morris' dream of artists and craftsmen working together in fruitful exchange. After Whitehead had failed in an earlier attempt to establish a community for furniture workers in Oregon, the possibilities of Woodstock were pointed out by Bolton Brown, an art educator from California. Meanwhile, a second philanthropist had become interested in the project when he met Whitehead at Hull House in Chicago. This was Hervey White, an Iowa born poet who had graduated from Harvard and later traveled through Italy. From the top of Mead Mountain the three men looked down on Woodstock's serene valleys. It seemed to them that the place perfectly fitted Ruskin's prescription for a spot where artists could function: mountains, but not too high and austere, and farmland rich with crops. And in its early and important glass-making industry, Woodstock already had a tradition of craftsmanship.

Woodstock had behind it a history rich in legend, folklore, and picturesque personalities. More recently it had become known for its tanneries, bluestone quarries, and Jonathan apples, but earlier it had been a center for the art of highly skilled glass makers, some reputedly kidnapped from Europe, whose capers were as colorful as any of the later generations of bohemians. (See also

Woodstock, An American Art Colony, 1902–1977, exhibition catalog, Vassar College Art Gallery, 1976, with introduction by Karal Ann Marling.)

Whitehead established his colony of craftsmen high up on a mountain he called Byrdcliffe, a combination of his own middle name and his wife's maiden name. For his own use and as a headquarters for the colony he built a spacious house at the top of the mountain, furnished it with Art Nouveau decor and simple hand-made furniture. Nearby, modest wooden cabins were constructed, equipped with looms, kilns for pottery making, benches for woodworking.

In the course of setting up the colony at Byrdcliffe it turned out that the poet's concept of an artists' Utopia was somewhat different: the "something untamed" that Hervey White associated with the artist was later embodied in a rearing wild horse carved by John Flannagan that became the emblem of the "Maverick," the name the poet gave to the one-hundred-acre plot of wooded land he bought in the valley. There he built at secluded intervals along a stream, a series of shacks he rented to painters and sculptors and writers for a token fee. A gentle, reticent person, White lived with a spartan simplicity that would impress today's "back to earth" cultists. For some years he reserved a small house for himself, later he turned over even this to the sculptor, Raoul Hague, who converted it into a studio home.

Philip Guston has lived for many years on the "Maverick." Many others who benefited from early stakes there have built their own homes in nearby sections of Woodstock. The colony now extends far beyond the early clusters.

A third art center was established in 1906 when the Art Students League opened a summer extension school there at the urging of Birge Harrison, a landscape painter who became the first of a number of well-known teachers (including the late Arnold Blanch who was responsible for the reopening of the school after a hiatus of two decades).

The simple life and communally shared creativity of medieval craftsmen (the ideal that inspired Ruskin and Morris) was never recreated on Byrdcliffe, but the high purpose of the philanthropist had a prolonged effect on the colony: the arts and crafts emphasis lingered for decades after Whitehead's looms and kilns were deserted (largely because of internal dissensions). Byrdcliffe became a center for opera. The selfless idealism of Hervey White made a deeper impression — without his dream Woodstock might have been just another artistic suburb.

Taos and Santa Fe

As a refuge from the rapacious commercial world, New Mexico had all the yearned-for requisites: unspoiled nature on a grand scale, man living free in a more primitive state, fascinating artifacts, mementos of ancient times, exotic rituals. The prospect of Indian adobes dwarfed by vast tablelands and massively convoluted mountains was made to order for artists with a bent for tailoring their picturesque tableaux to the demands of Eastern markets.

There were deeper, more human satisfactions too. At a time when industrial "progress" was devouring the wilderness at a staggering pace, New Mexico seemed timeless; it promised to hold out longer (a deceptive promise, it turned out after World War II). Artists feeling themselves in a materialistic society in some ways almost as much ignored as the Indian could group together for mutual support. About 100 had arrived by 1915. For some serious artists deeply drawn to the place, a sojourn proved sadly disappointing: they found it impossible to integrate the scale and grandeur of the landscape into their personal outlook and formal vocabulary.

A very few were able to dig beneath the surface picturesqueness and develop the formal means to convey the reality they found. As early as the 1880's individual painters had stopped in Taos to record the landscape; by the early 1900's a group, some of whom had met in Paris, were settling into summer residences there and also a little later in Santa Fe. They were mostly academically skilled painters trained abroad and oriented to building their careers on the exploitation of exotic subject matter.

One of the earliest and best-known founders of the colony, Ernest Blumenschien (his friend, Joseph Sharp was the first to "discover" Taos and extoll its attractions in Paris) wrote of their motivation: "We were ennuied with the hackneyed subject matter of thousands of painters; windmills in a Dutch landscape, Brittany peasants with sabots, French roads lined with Normandy poplars, lady in negligée reclining on a sumptuous divan...We felt the need of a stimulating subject." A third member of the trio of young Americans who found Taos by way of Paris was Bert Phillips, steeped in romanticism; other expatriates followed. They all relied on magazine illustration as well as the sale of studio work. Sharp's work with its objective, authentic reporting of Indian tribal life, is collected today as a valuable ethnological record.

. Paul Burlin went to Santa Fe in 1913, the same year he exhibited in the Armory Show that introduced modern art to the U.S. He was the first artist with the imagination to tap the fertile resource of Indian art, extracting from it the rhythms he could relate to the innovations of the European moderns. The vitality of his early style owes much to abstract elements he studied in Indian arts along with their music.

Andrew Dasburg who went to Taos in 1917, became a permanent resident in the 1930's. He interpreted the landscape in a Cezannesque geometry. In 1918 Marsden Hartley produced vigorous still-life paintings including Santos; four years later in Germany he was still painting his recollections of mountain and plain.

Stuart Davis expressed a sense of failure after a frustrated summer of trying to paint in Santa Fe in 1923. "(I) did not do much work because the place itself was so interesting. I don't think you could do much work there except in a literal way. You always have to look at it. Then there's the great dead population. You don't see them but you stumble over them. It's a place for an ethnologist, not an artist." Edward Hopper, a summer visitor in 1925, managed only a watercolor of an old locomotive on his first trip.

In the 1920's and 1930's the focus of artists in the now-expanded colonies shifted from Indians to the landscape itself and to a search for fresh formal means. In the one hundred watercolors he produced in one summer (1929) at Taos, John Marin offered a dramatic example of how a constructive imagination and expressionist brush could combine to convey the vast spaces and tumultuous energies of the country.

But it remained for Georgia O'Keefe to distill from the land its most pure and elemental quality. Settling first in Taos, later making her home at Abiquiu, she turned her attention to those remains of the dead that Stuart Davis had complained he was always stumbling upon and proved they could be claimed by the artist as well as the ethnologist. Stripped of all superficially picturesque elements, a bleached animal skull, a Hispanic cross, or the fluidly sculptured adobe wall of a native church could project a mysterious unity of objective place and the subjective person. (See also *Taos and Santa Fe: The Artists Environment...1882–1942* by Van Deren Coke (ex. cat.) Albuquerque, New Mexico 1963.)

Easthampton

In the 1870's Easthampton, near the outermost tip of Long Island, was an attractive sketching area for painters of picturesque landscape, but the town and its ocean beaches became better known after 1878 when it was adopted as a summer retreat by Elihu Vedder, Winslow Homer, J. Alden Weir, John Twachtman, Sanford White and other illustrious members of the Tile Club, a socially cohesive group whose hobby of painting on Spanish tiles brought them together in New York on Wednesday nights. Regulars in the early decades of the twentieth century were Childe Hassam and Thomas Moran who founded the Maidenstone Club. In 1931 The Guild Hall was inaugurated, and two years later the Amagansett Art School was launched by Hilton Leech.

In the 1940's Easthampton was summer host to a distinguished group of European emigrés taking refuge in the United States from Hitler and World War II, among them: Fernand Léger, Max Ernst, Jean Helion, Matta and an earlier arrival, Marcel Duchamp. Many of them were invited to the colony by socialite art patrons, Sara and Gerald Murphy, whose home on the Riviera had been open to Picasso and many other modern artists. (Gerald Murphy also painted in a crisp, collage-like style now seen by some critics as anticipating Pop Art.) The Guild Hall initiated its *Artists of the Region* exhibits in 1949 and in the 1950's the Sigma Gallery on Main Street also showed the work of contemporaries.

An influx of avant-garde artists, some of international stature, and their followers and sympathetic critics, was ushered in after Lee Krasner and Jackson Pollock acquired a house and studio-barn at Springs in 1945. It was the beginning of a decade in which the rising financial fortunes of the Abstract Expressionists in particular, funded the building or acquisition of substantial homes and elaborately equipped studios. Among them were Willem de Kooning, Adolph Gottlieb, Robert Motherwell, Alfonso Ossorio, Mark Rothko, James Brooks, Conrad Marca-Relli, Grace Hartigan. Adolph Gottlieb, who moved there from Provincetown in the late 1950's, said that Easthampton was the place for the established artist. (See also *Artists and Easthampton, A 100 Year Perspective,* exhibition catalog, Museum Section, Guild Hall of Easthampton, East Hampton, N.Y., Aug. 14–Oct. 3, 1976.)

Gloucester and Rockport (Cape Ann)

Decades before artists discovered Provincetown, some of America's most distinguished landscapists were painting the rugged coast of Gloucester and the fishing port of more northerly Cape Ann. As described by John Wilmerding: "Soft, deep-curved beaches alternate with high cliffs and ledges, all rimmed with an endless variety of rocks and dramatically emphasized by extreme tidal changes."

Gloucester benefited from no founding group fired by a dream of an artists' Utopia. It entered art history through the work of an extraordinarily gifted native son whose paintings of its rugged coast are now receiving wider recognition. Born in Gloucester in 1804, Fitz Hugh Lane was largely self-taught. Possibly because he was partially crippled he did not manage the trip to Europe for training then considered essential. After working in Boston as a lithographer, he returned home in 1848 and spent the rest of his life (he died in 1865) painting the scene with delicacy and precision in a style recently defined as "luminism." With a sharp-focus rendition of the mass and structure of rocks and matchless architecture of the Gloucester schooner, he also favored a pervasive late-afternoon light that invested the subject with a quiet mystery. The appealingly primitive aspects of his work were accentuated by his preference for panoramic views with no foreground shapes (an effect he apparently obtained by sketching from an offshore rowboat).

James F. O'Gorman, authority on the artists of Cape Ann, summed up the importance of Gloucester in the work of some who followed Fitz Hugh Lane: "These artists had traveled the world ... yet they were drawn some time during their careers to explore, as Stuart Davis put it, 'the rocks, moors, and docks of Cape Ann.' In the cases of Duveneck, Twachtman, and Hunt their Gloucester summers were the capstones of distinguished careers. For Davis, Homer and Sloan, Gloucester played a key role in their artistic development."

Winslow Homer probably saw the paintings of Fitz Hugh Lane while he was working as a graphic artist in Boston. He first came to Gloucester in the summer of 1873 when he was beginning to use watercolor, largely in studies of subjects to be developed in oils. When he returned in 1880 he was handling watercolor with a respect for the medium itself and in full command of its fluidity and transparency. That summer he painted *The Green Dory* and *Children Playing Under a Gloucester Wharf*.

In 1877 Europe-trained William Morris Hunt exclaimed: "I believe that I have painted a picture with *light* in it." He had just painted *Gloucester Harbor* out of doors in a single afternoon using an atmospheric style patterned after Millet and the Barbizon artists. He was the first of a series of Impressionistically-inclined painters who were to follow: John Henry Twachtman, around 1900, Childe Hassam in the teens, and Frank Duvenick around 1910 in a more tonal variation.

During the years of World War I, John Sloan spent five summers painting the scene with bright colors and a loose brush that may have reflected the impact of the Post-Impressionists at the 1913 Armory Show. In a vein more reminiscent of the street scenes of his association with the "Ash Can School" he also painted *Gloucester Trolley* in 1917. At the suggestion of Sloan, Stuart Davis came to Gloucester in 1915 and worked there, except for several summers of travel, until 1934. Another modern, Marsden Hartley, painted the ice-age boulders of Dogtown in the early 1930's.

Although Gloucester was becoming crowded with art students, many artists, modern and traditional, were to find what isolation they needed in the decades that followed. The Cape Ann communities never developed the clubs and concentration of forums, galleries, and theater groups that can still make a Provincetown summer both stimulating and exhausting. But in 1916 John Sloan found Gloucester too crowded. He quipped: "There was an artist's shadow beside ever cow in Gloucester, and the cows themselves were dying of eating paint rags."

D.G.S.

PROVINCETOWN PAINTERS

Anonymous

"Provincetown Harbor" c. 1877
pastel on paper   23½" × 14½"
Collection of Mr. James Simpson
Provincetown, Massachusetts

114

A. Acores
American
"Arbitrator" 1906
watercolor on paper   23½" × 14½"
Collection of Mr. James Simpson
Provincetown, Massachusetts

115

Anonymous
American

"Lizzie Matheson," c. 1890

oil on canvas   21½" × 35½"

Collection of Nancy O. Merrill
Provincetown, Massachusetts

116

Anonymous

"Whaling Scene"

oil on canvas   19½" × 14½"

Collection of Mr. James Simpson
Provincetown, Massachusetts

William F. Halsall

b. 1841, Kirkdale, England   d. 1919
active in Provincetown, 1890's –1919

"Peaked Hills of Cape Cod,"

oil on canvas   36" × 50"

Collection of the Town of Provincetown
Provincetown, Massachusetts
Gift of Mary Elizabeth Smith

Charles Hawthorne

b. 1872, Richmond, Maine   d. 1930
active in Provincetown, 1915–1930

"Bums Drinking"

oil on canvas   40″ × 30″

Collection of the Coe Kerr Gallery
New York, New York

Charles Hawthorne
b. 1872, Richmond, Maine   d. 1930
active in Provincetown, 1915–1930

"The First Voyage"

oil on canvas   4' × 5'

Collection of the Provincetown Art Association
Provincetown, Massachusetts

120

Charles Hawthorne
b. 1872, Richmond, Maine   d. 1930
active in Provincetown, 1915–1930

"Men Cleaning Fish"

oil on canvas   5′ × 4′

Collection of the Town of Provincetown
Provincetown, Massachusetts

121

Childe Hassam

**b. 1859, Dorchester, Massachusetts   d. 1935
active in Provincetown, 1900–1901**

"Provincetown Grocery Store," 1902

oil on canvas   21¾" × 17¾"

Collection of the Santa Barbara Museum of Art, Santa Barbara, California
Bequest of Mrs. Stanley R. McCormick in
memory of her husband Stanley R. McCormick

122

Childe Hassam

**b. 1859, Dorchester, Massachusetts   d. 1935
active in Provincetown, 1900–1901**

"Provincetown," 1900

oil on canvas   24″ × 23″

Collection of Canajoharie Library and Art Gallery
Canajoharie, New York

Roswell S. Hill
American, 1861–1907
"Provincetown Harbor"
oil on canvas   21⅛″ × 21⁴/₈″
Collection of Everson Museum
Syracuse, New York

124

Ernest Lawson

**b. 1873, Halifax, Nova Scotia d. 1939
active in Provincetown, 1920**

"Sea Coast, Cape Cod," 1915
25⅛" × 30¼"

Collection of the University of Nebraska-Lincoln Art Galleries
Lincoln, Nebraska

William Paxton
b. 1869, Boston, Massachusetts   d. 1941
active in Provincetown, 1916–1940

"Little Girl with a Parasol," 1908

oil on canvas   27″ × 22″

Collection of Robert Douglas Hunter
Boston, Massachusetts

Richard Miller
b. 1875, St. Louis, Missouri   d. 1943
active in Provincetown, 1915–1943

"Reverie"

oil on canvas   36" × 34"

Collection of the Museum of Art, Rhode Island
School of Design. Gift of Mrs. William C. Baker
Providence, Rhode Island

127

Arthur Diehl
American

"Provincetown" 1913

oil on canvas   25½" × 13½"

Collection of Ruth Hiebert
Provincetown, Massachusetts

128

Coulton Waugh

b. 1869, St. Ives, Cornwall, England   d. 1973
Active in Provincetown 1925–1943

"Old Whale Ship Drying Sails," 1931

oil on canvas   42⅛" × 50⅛"

Collection of First National Bank of Cape Cod
Orleans, Massachusetts

Charles Heinz

b. 1885, Shelbyville, Illinois   d. 1953
active in Provincetown, 1929–1953

"Oyster Shacks, Wellfleet"

oil on canvas   28 6/8″ × 35″

Collection of the Provincetown Art Association
Provincetown, Massachusetts

130

Ambrose Webster
b. 1869, Charlestown, Massachusetts   d. 193
active in Provincetown 1900–1935

"Red House," Provincetown, 1920

oil on canvas   20" × 24"

Collection of Babcock Galleries
New York, New York

Ambrose Webster

**b. 1869, Charlestown, Massachusetts   d. 1935
active in Provincetown 1900–1935**

"Tamworth New Hampshire," 1914

oil on canvas   28½" × 38½"

Collection of Babcock Galleries
New York, New York

132

John Noble
b. 1874, Witchita, Kansas   d. 1934
active in Provincetown, 1919–1934

"Sardine Fishermen," 1920

Oil on canvas   36″ × 30″

Collection of the Milch Galleries
New York, New York

John Noble
b. 1874, Witchita, Kansas   d. 1934
active in Provincetown, 1919–1934

"Pink Cloud"

oil on canvas   23" × 27"

Collection of Ruth Hiebert
Provincetown, Massachusetts

134

Max Bohm
b. 1868, Cleveland, Ohio d. 1923
active in Provincetown, 1916–1923

"Gathering Clouds"

oil on canvas   19¾" × 24"

Collection of Elizabeth Schwartz and Esther Locke
Provincetown, Massachusetts

Frederick Waugh
b. 1861, Bordentown, New Jersey   d. 1940
active in Provincetown, 1916–1940

"Looking Seaward"

oil on canvas   52″ × 44″

Collection of Syracuse University Art Collection
Syracuse, New York

136

Gerrit Beneker

b. 1882, Grand Rapids, Michigan   d. 1934
active in Provincetown, 1915–1934

"Icebound, Provincetown"

oil on canvas   34½″ × 34½″

Collection of Mr. and Mrs. Lawrence Gates
Providence, Rhode Island

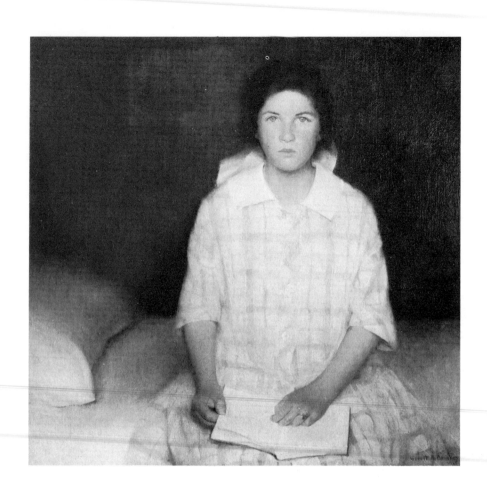

Gerrit Beneker

b. 1882, Grand Rapids, Michigan   d. 1934
active in Provincetown, 1915–1934

"End of the Story," 1915

oil on canvas   34" × 34"

Collection of Mr. and Mrs. Leonard Granoff
Providence, Rhode Island

Gerrit Beneker

b. 1882, Grand Rapids, Michigan   d. 1934
active in Provincetown, 1915–1934

"Fisherman of Truro," 1918

oil on canvas   33½″ × 33½″

Collection of Mr. and Mrs. Lawrence Gates
Providence, Rhode Island

Reynolds Beal
b. 1867, New York, N.Y.   d. 1951
active in Provincetown 1900–1919

"Provincetown Waterfront," 1916

oil on canvas   29″ × 36″

Collection of Vose Galleries of Boston
Boston, Massachusetts

Gifford Beal

b. 1879, New York, New York   d. 1956
active in Provincetown, 1946–1950

"Circus Scene"

oil on canvas   16″ × 20″

Collection of the Kraushaar Galleries
New York, New York

George Elmer Browne

**b. 1871, Gloucester, Massachusetts   d. 1945
active in Provincetown, 1919–1945**

"Fishing Boats, Provincetown"

oil on canvas   15″ × 18″

Collection of Chapellier Galleries, Inc.
New York, New York

142

Edwin Reeves Euler
b. 1896, DeLamar, Nevada
active in Provincetown 1919–present
"Conwell Street Railroad Crossing" 1932
oil on canvas   25″ × 30″
Collection of the artist
Provincetown, Massachusetts

Vollian B. Rann

**b. 1897, Wilmington, North Carolina d. 1956
active in Provincetown, 1922–1956**

"Manuel Gaspar"   *34" × 38"*

Collection of Mr. Edward L. Shein
Providence, Rhode Island

144

Edwin Dickinson

b. 1891, Seneca Falls, New York
active in Provincetown, 1912–present

"An Anniversary" 1921

oil on canvas   60″ × 72″

Collection of the Albright-Knox Art Gallery
Buffalo, New York

Philip C. Malicoat

b. 1908, Indianapolis, Indiana
active in Provincetown, 1929–present

"Peaked Hill Coast Guard Station" 1958

oil on canvas   16" × 20"

Collection of the artist
Provincetown, Massachusetts

146

Henry Hensche
b. 1901, Chicago, Illinois
active in Provincetown, 1922–present

"Fall Landscape," 1941

oil on canvas   16" × 20"

Collection of the artist
Provincetown, Massachusetts

William Draper

**b. 1912, Hopedale, Massachusetts
active in Provincetown 1929–1932**

"Backyard Provincetown 1932," 1932

oil on canvas   36" × 30"

Collection of the artist
New York, New York

148

George Yater
b. 1910, Madison, Indiana
active in Provincetown, 1931–present
"Pond Village – Springtime," 1940
oil on canvas   30″ × 36″
Collection of George Yater
Truro, Massachusetts

Bruce McKain

b. 1900, Freetown, Indiana
active in Provincetown, 1928–present

"Virgin Snow," 1974

oil on canvas   25" × 30"

Collection of the artist
Provincetown, Massachusetts

150

Ross Moffett
b. 1888, Clearfield, Iowa   d. 1971
active in Provincetown, 1913–1971

"Gull Hill," 1929

oil on canvas   48″ × 60″

Collection of Elizabeth Moffett Johnson
Provincetown, Massachusetts

Ross Moffett
b. 1888, Clearfield, Iowa   d. 1971
active in Provincetown, 1913–1971

"Shank Painter Pond," 1925

oil on canvas   30" × 40"

Collection of the Town of Provincetown
Provincetown, Massachusetts

152

Pauline Palmer
b. McHenry, Illinois
active in Provincetown, 1920's, 1930's

"The Artist's Studio"

clear glass   15½" × 19½"

Collection of Mrs. Daniel Herbert
Provincetown, Massachusetts

Jo N. Hopper
active in Provincetown, 1930–1967
"Methodist Church, Provincetown," 1947
watercolor on paper   19½" × 13½"
Collection of the Whitney Museum of American Art
New York, New York
Bequest of Josephine N. Hopper

154

John Whorf

**b. 1903, Winthrop, Massachusetts   d. 1959
active in Provincetown 1905–1959**

"Mallard Ducks Coasting Home," 1950

30″ × 22½″

Collection of Mrs. Courtney Allen
North Truro, Massachusetts

Courtney Allen

b. 1895, Norfolk, Virginia   d. 1969
active in Provincetown, 1919–1969

"Dead Woodcock," 1962

oil on canvas   11″ × 15″

Collection of Mrs. Courtney Allen
North Truro, Massachusetts

156

Peter Hunt

**b. 1898, New York, New York   d. 1969
active in Provincetown, 1930–1960**

painted chest, 1960

Collection of Mr. & Mrs. Fred Lerman
Syracuse, New York

B. J. O. Nordfelt
b. 1878, Sweden   d. 1955
active in Provincetown, 1916–early 1920's

"Bathers" 1916

oil on canvas   24″ × 30″

Collection of Provincetown Art Association
Provincetown, Massachusetts

158

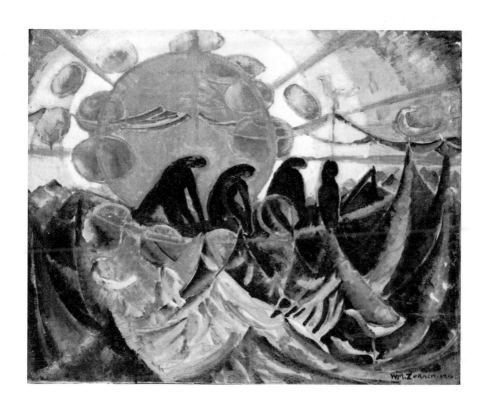

William Zorach

b. 1887, Eurburg, Lithuania   d. 1966
active in Provincetown, 1914, 1916, 1921

"Hauling the Weir – Provincetown," 1916

oil on canvas   24" × 29"

Collection of Zabriskie Gallery
New York, New York

Agnes Weinrich
b. Iowa   d. 1940
"Still Life"
watercolor   17″ × 14½″
Collection of Mr. Edward L. Shein
Providence, Rhode Island

160

Blanche Lazell
b. Maidsville, Virginia   d. 1956
active in Provincetown, 1916–1956

"Painting #12," 1929

Oil on board   30″ × 30″

Collection of the Provincetown Art Association
Provincetown, Massachusetts

161

Marsden Hartley
b. 1877, Lewiston, Maine   d. 1943
active in Provincetown, 1917

"Trixie," 1916

oil on board   24″ × 20″

Collection of Mrs. Harriet W. Heron

Henry Varnum Poor

b. 1888, Chapman, Kansas   d. 1970
active in Provincetown, 1933–1970

"South Truro Hills," 1950

watercolor and tempera on paper   14″ × 17″

Collection of the Frank Rehn Gallery
New York, New York

Abraham Walkowitz

**b. 1878, Tumen, U.S.S.R. d. 1965
active in Provincetown, 1916, 1929, 1932**

"View of Provincetown Rooftops" 1912

watercolor   11½″ × 15½″

Collection of Zabriskie Gallery
New York, New York

164

George Ault
b. 1891, Cleveland, Ohio d. 1948
active in Provincetown, 1922–1927

"The Green Fish House," 1921
watercolor on paper   14″ × 10″
Collection of Coe Kerr Gallery
New York, New York

Charles Demuth

b. 1873, Lancaster, Pennsylvania d. 1935
active in Provincetown, 1914, 1919–20, 1930

"Early Houses, Provincetown," 1918

watercolor on paper   14″ × 10″

Collection of the Museum of Modern Art, New York, New York
Gift of Phillip L. Goodwin

Charles Demuth

b. 1873, Lancaster, Pennsylvania   d. 1935
active in Provincetown, 1914, 1919–20, 1930

"Sailboats, Provincetown," 1916

watercolor on paper   9½″ × 13⅝″

Collection of Carolyn Wose Hull
State College, Pennsylvania

167

Niles Spencer

b. 1893, Pawtucket, Rhode Island   d. 1952
active in Provincetown 1924–1940

"New England Landscape" 1924

oil on canvas   22″ × 35″

Collection of Albright-Knox Art Gallery, Charles Goodyear Fund
Buffalo, New York

Maurice Sterne
b. 1877, Libau, U.S.S.R.   d. 1957
active in Provincetown, 1915–1947

"Still Life," 1925

oil on canvas   42″ × 38″

Collection of Babcock Galleries
New York, New York

Stuart Davis

**b. 1894, Philadelphia, Pennsylvania   d. 1964
active in Provincetown, 1913**

"Graveyard on the Dunes," 1913

oil on canvas   38″ × 30″

Collection of Mrs. Roselle Davis
New York, New York

170

Raphael Soyer
b. 1899, U.S.S.R.
active in Provincetown, 1928–30, 1954, 1957
1974–1975.

"Railroad Yard," 1930

oil on canvas   18¼" × 24¼"

Collection of Raphael Soyer
New York, New York

Robert D. Hunter

b. 1928, Boston, Massachusetts
active in Provincetown, 1949–present

"Station Agent," 1968

oil on panel   26" × 20"

Collection of Mrs. R. D. Hunter   artist's
Boston, Massachusetts

172

R. H. Ives Gammel

b. 1893, Providence, Rhode Island
active in Provincetown 1915–1968

"The Fruit Stand" 1939

oil on canvas   40″ × 30″

Collection of the Chrysler Art Museum at Norfolk
Norfolk, Virginia

Jerry Farnsworth
b. 1895, Dalton, Georgia
active in Provincetown 1915–1972

"Girl in Red Shirt"

oil on canvas   29″ × 26″

Collection of Mr. and Mrs. Jerry Farnsworth
Sarasota, Florida

174

Helen Farnsworth Sawyer
b. 1900, Washington, D.C.
active in Provincetown, 1927, 1954–1972

"Pamet River"

oil on canvas   36½″ × 29½″

Collection of Mr. & Mrs. Jerry Farnsworth
Sarasota, Florida

James Wingate Parr

b. 1923, Boston, Massachusetts   d. 1969
active in Provincetown, 1948–1969

"Two Dead Crows"

oil on canvas   80″ × 65″

Collection of Mr. James Simpson
Truro, Massachusetts

176

Lodewyk Bruckman

b. 1913, The Hague, Holland
active in Provincetown, 1953–early 1960's

"The Shirt" (Portrait of James Simpson)
1951–1955

oil on canvas   27" × 37"

Collection of Mr. James Simpson
Truro, Massachusetts

177

J. Oppenheimer
American
"Rainy Day at Provincetown" 1953
watercolor on paper   18″ × 12″
Collection of Mr. and Mrs. Leonard Granoff
Providence, Rhode Island

178

Byron Browne
b. 1907, Yonkers, New York   d. 1961
active in Provincetown, 1952–1961

"Provincetown Beach," 1956

oil on canvas   16″ × 30″

Collection of Mr. and Mrs. Lawrence Richmond
Great Neck, New York

Paul Burlin

b. 1886, New York, N.Y.   d. 1969
active in Provincetown, early 1930's, late 1950's, and late 1960's

"New England Landscape," 1921

oil on canvas   29" × 36"

Collection of Borgenicht Gallery
New York, New York

180

Chaim Gross
b. 1904, Kolomea, East Austria
active in Provincetown, 1924, 1938, 1939
1943–present

"Early Morning Fishermen," 1951
watercolor and drawing   14½" × 22½"
Collection of Everson Museum
Syracuse, New York

181

Chaim Gross

b. 1904, Kolomea, East Austria
active in Provincetown, 1924, 1938, 1939,
1943–present

"Provincetown Fisherman on Pier" 1953

watercolor on paper   29" × 23"

Collection of Forum Gallery
New York, New York

182

Ben Shahn
b. 1898, Kovno, Lithuania d. 1969
active in Provincetown, 1925–1935

"Truro Bathers," 1931–1932

watercolor   22" × 15"

Collection of Judith Shahn Dugan and Ezra Shahn
Boulder, Colorado

Ben Shahn

b. 1898, Kovno, Lithuania   d. 1969
active in Provincetown, 1925–1935

"Demonstration" 1933 (Tom Mooney Series)

gouache on gesso board   23½" × 17"

Collection of Judith Shahn Dugan and Ezra Shahn
Boulder, Colorado

184

Sol Wilson

b. 1897, Vilmo, Poland   d. 1974
active in Provincetown 1947–1974

"Fisherman's Family," 1946

oil on canvas   25" × 30"

Collection of Babcock Galleries
New York, New York

Karl Knaths

b. 1891, EauClaire, Wisconsin   d. 1971
active in Provincetown, 1919–1971

"Number O–Adam," 1948

oil on canvas   41" × 50½"

Collection of the Albright-Knox Gallery
Room of Contemporary Art Fund
New York, New York

186

Karl Knaths
b. 1891, EauClaire, Wisconsin   d. 1971
active in Provincetown, 1919–1971

"Sail Loft," 1965

oil on canvas   40″ × 50″

Collection of the Syracuse University Art Collection
Syracuse, New York

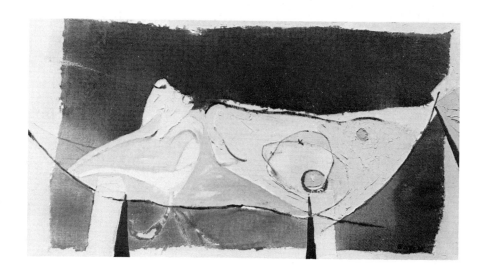

Lee Gatch

**b. 1902, Baltimore, Maryland   d. 1968
active in Provincetown 1930–1940's**

"The Bovine Tapestry" 1958

oil on canvas   19⅝″ × 35⅝″

Collection of the Colgate University Art Collection
Hamilton, New York
(Gift of Herbert Mayer, Class of 1929)

188

Milton Avery
b. 1893, Altmar, New York   d. 1965
active in Provincetown, 1956, 1960

"Sail," 1958

oil on canvas   72" × 50"

Collection of Milton Avery Trust
New York, New York

189

Morris Kantor
b. 1896, Minsk, U.S.S.R.   d. 1974
active in Provincetown, 1932

"Dunes at Sunset," 1939

oil on canvas   26″ × 30″

Collection of Mrs. Martha Kantor
New City, New York

190

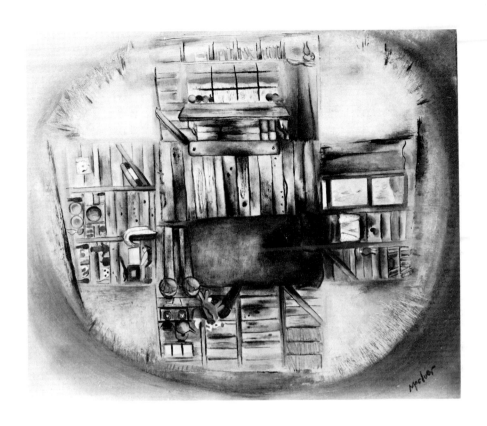

Loren MacIver
b. 1909, New York, New York
active in Provincetown, 1930–1938

"The Shack," 1934

oil on canvas   20⅛" × 24"

Collection of the Museum of Modern Art, New York, New York
Gift of Abby Aldrich Rockefeller, 1938

Edward Hopper

b. 1882, Nyack, New York   d. 1967
active in Provincetown, 1930–1967

"The Camel's Hump," 1931

oil on canvas   32¼" × 50⅛"

Collection of the Munson-Williams-Proctor Institute
Edward W. Root Bequest
Utica, New York

192

Edward Hopper

b. 1882, Nyack, New York   d. 1967
active in Provincetown, 1930–1967

"Cape Cod Sunset," 1934

oil on canvas   28⅞" × 35⅞"

Collection of the Whitney Museum of American Art
New York, New York
Bequest of Josephine N. Hopper

George Grosz
b. 1893 Berlin, Germany   d. 1959
active in Provincetown, 1937–1945

"Cape Cod Farm," 1939

watercolor on paper   13½″ × 18″

Collection of Mr. and Mrs. Albin White
Inglewood Cliffs, New Jersey

194

George Grosz
b. 1893, Berlin, Germany   d. 1959
active in Provincetown, 1937–1945

"Gold and Blue Bay," 1939

watercolor onnpaper   18″ × 13½″

Collection of Mr. and Mrs. Albin H. White
Inglewood Cliffs, New Jersey

Oliver Newberry Chaffee
b. 1881, Detroit, Michigan   d. 1944
Active in Provincetown, 1913–1944

"Cruxifiction," 1933

oil on cotton canvas   72" × 48"

Collection of the Provincetown Heritage Museum
Provincetown, Massachusetts

196

Richard Florsheim
b. 1916, Chicago, Illinois
active in Provincetown 1954–present

"Beach Light" 1977

oil on canvas   12″ × 36″

Collection of the A.C.A. Gallery
New York, New York

Gerrit Hondius

**b. 1891, Kampen, Holland   d. 1970
active in Provincetown, 1952–1970**

"Still Life," 1968

oil on canvas   31⅜" × 41⅜"

Gift of Mrs. Paula Hondius
Collection of Everson Museum
Syracuse, New York

198

Salvatore Del Deo

b. 1928, Providence, Rhode Island
active in Provincetown, 1946–present

"Cape Cod Cold Storage," 1968

oil on canvas   20″ × 24″

Collection of the Provincetown Heritage Museum
Provincetown, Massachusetts

Joe Kaplan
b. 1900, Minsk, U.S.S.R.
active in Provincetown, early 1920's–present

"Stormy Sea"

oil on canvas   30″ × 40″

Collection of the artist
Provincetown, Massachusetts

200

Mary Cecil Allen
b. 1893, Australia   d. 1960's
active in Provincetown, 1950's, 1960's

Untitled

collage   15½″ × 16½″

Collection of Mr. and Mrs. Nicholas Wells
Provincetown, Massachusetts

201

Anne Brigadier

b. 1908, New York, N.Y.
active in Provincetown, 1940–present

"Sunset Glow"

encaustic collage   18″ × 14″

Collection of the artist
New York, New York

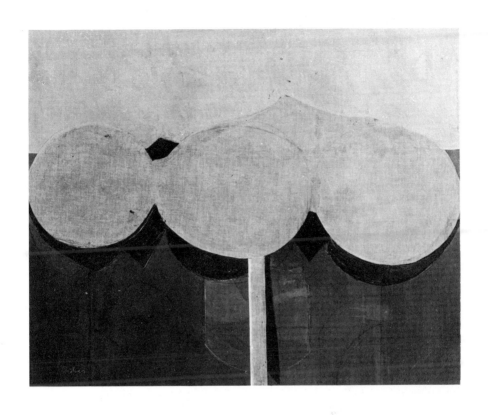

Henry Botkin

b. 1896, Boston, Massachusetts
active in Provincetown, 1950–present

"The Drums" 1967

oil and cloth collage on masonite   30″ × 33½″

Collection of the Syracuse University Art Collection
Syracuse, New York

Lillian Orlowsky

b. 1914, New York, New York
active in Provincetown, 1938, 1945–present

"Woman"

collage   15½″ × 24¾″

Collection of the artist
New York, New York

204

Leo Manso
b. 1914, New York, New York
active in Provincetown, 1947–present

"Thomas–a Becket," 1964
assemblage   48″ × 36″

Collection of Blanche Manso
New York, New York

Weldon Kees

**b. 1914, Beatrice, Nebraska   d. 1955
active in Provincetown, 1949**

Untitled

watercolor, guache, and wat   25½″ × 22¼″

Collection of the University of Nebraska, Lincoln Art Gallery
Lincoln, Nebraska

206

William Baziotes

**b. 1912, Pittsburgh, Pennsylvania   d. 1963
active in Provincetown, 1946–1950**

"Underground," 1945

pastel and pencil on paper   17¼" × 11¼"

Collection of Marlborough Gallery
New York, New York

207

Adolph Gottlieb

b. 1903, New York, New York d. 1974
active in Provincetown 1946–1958

Untitled

gouache on paper   20″ × 26″

Gift of Andre Emmerica
Collection of Everson Museum
Syracuse, New York

208

Adolph Gottlieb
b. 1903, New York, New York   d. 1974
active in Provincetown 1946–1958

"Low Tide" 1949

oil and tempera on canvas   38″ × 30″

Collection of Mrs. Adolph Gottlieb
New York, New York

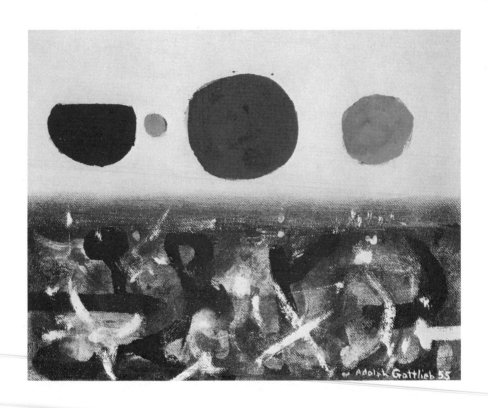

Adolph Gottlieb
b. 1903, New York, New York   d. 1974
active in Provincetown 1946–1958

"Imaginary Landscape" 1955

oil on canvas   8″ × 10″

Collection of Mr. Lawrence Richmond
Great Neck, New York

210

Lee Krasner
b. 1911, Brooklyn, New York
active in Provincetown, 1938–1944

Untitled, 1930's
oil on canvas   29¾″ × 24″
Collection of Jason McCoy
New York, New York

Peter Busa
b. 1914, Pittsburgh, Pennsylvania
active in Provincetown, 1936–1970

"Star Gazers," 1940

oil on canvas   72″ × 84″

Collection of the artist
Minneapolis, Minnesota

212

Will Barnet

**b. 1911, Beverly, Massachusetts
active in Provincetown, 1956–1958**

"Clear Day," 1956

oil on canvas   44″ × 36″

Collection of the Allentown Art Museum
Allentown, Pennsylvania

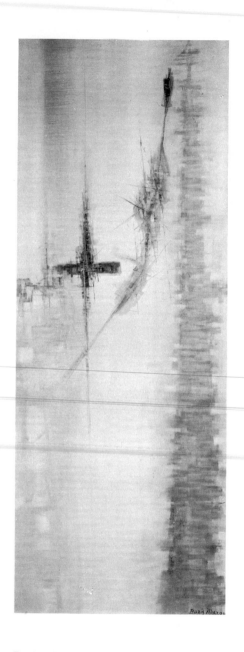

Boris Margo

b. 1902, Wolotschisk, U.S.S.R.
active in Provincetown, 1949–present

"From Outward Flight"

oil on canvas   65″ × 25″
Collection of Lawrence Richmond
Great Neck, New York

214

Hans Hofmann

b. 1880, Weissenberg, Bavaria   d. 1966
active in Provincetown, 1932–1966

"Landscape," 1936

oil on canvas   30″ × 36″

Collection of the Andre Emmerich Gallery
New York, New York

Hans Hofmann

**b. 1880, Weissenberg, Bavaria   d. 1966
active in Provincetown, 1932–1966**

"Landscape," 1935

oil on plywood   30″ × 36″

Collection of the Andre Emmerich Gallery
New York, New York

216

Hans Hofmann

b. 1880, Weissenberg, Bavaria   d. 1966
active in Provincetown, 1932–1966

"Heraldic Call," 1959

oil on canvas   40″ × 50″

Collection of Mr. and Mrs. Robert Peter Miller
New York, New York

217

John Grillo

**b. 1917, Lawrence, Massachusetts
active in Provincetown 1949–present**

"Sunburst" 1963

oil on canvas   60″ × 50″
Collection of the artist
Amherst, Massachusetts

218

James E. Gahagan, Jr.
b. 1927, New York, New York
active in Provincetown 1949, 1950, 1952–present

"September Song" 1957

oil on linen canvas   25″ × 30″

Collection of the artist
Plainfield, Vermont

Jim Forsberg
b. 1919, Sauk Center, Minnesota
active in Provincetown 1953–present

"Nocturne" 1960

oil on canvas   50″ × 36″

Collection of the Syracuse University Art Collection
Syracuse, New York

220

Morris Davidson
b. 1898, Rochester, New York
active in Provincetown, 1925–present

"Mexican Hat," 1954

oil on canvas   24" × 20"

Collection of Mr. Lawrence Richmond
Great Neck, New York

William Freed
b. 1902, Poland
active in Provincetown 1945–present
Untitled
oil on canvas   32″ × 42″
Collection of the artist
New York, New York

222

Stephen Pace
b. 1918, Charleston, Missouri
active in Provincetown, 1956–1966

"59 A-14," 1959

oil on canvas   59″ × 51″

Collection of the artist
Washington, D.C.

223

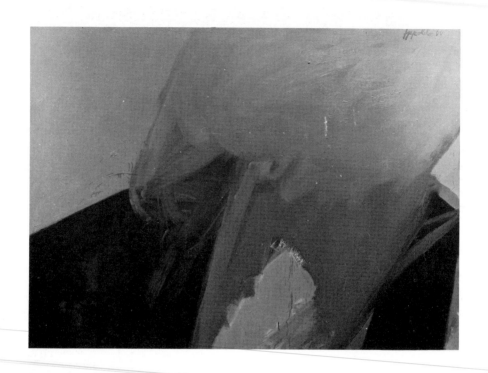

Angelo Ippolito
b. 1922, St. Arsenio, Italy
active in Provincetown, 1956–1965

"Big F.," 1960

oil on canvas   60″ × 79″
Collection of the artist
Binghamton, New York

224

Georgio Cavallon
b. 1904, Sorlo, Italy
active in Provincetown, 1927–present

Untitled, 1964

oil on canvas   17¼″ × 16″

Collection of the Gruenebaum Gallery
New York, New York

Sabina Teichman
b. New York, New York
active in Provincetown 1934–present

"Fragment – 1977"

oil on canvas   20" × 24"

Collection of Sabina Teichman
New York, New York

226

Franz Kline
b. 1910, Wilkes-Barre, Pennsylvania   d. 1962
active in Provincetown, late 50's–1962

"Coal Valley," 1957

brush and oil on board, collage   14 6/8″ × 11 2/8″

Collection of the Estate of Franz Kline
New York, New York

Franz Kline

b. 1910, Wilkes-Barre, Pennsylvania   d. 1962
active in Provincetown, late 50's–1962

"Untitled"

tempera on Brooklyn telephone book page   11″ × 9″

Collection of the Estate of Franz Kline
New York, New York

228

Franz Kline

**b. 1910, Wilkes-Barre, Pennsylvania   d. 1962
active in Provincetown, late 50's–1962**

"Untitled"

tempera or ink on Manhattan telephone book page   11″ × 9″

Collection of the Estate of Franz Kline
New York, New York

Helen Frankenthaler

b. 1928, New York, New York
active in Provincetown 1957–1969

"The Human Edge" 1967

acrylic on canvas   10′ 4″ × 93¼″

Museum Purchase
Collection of Everson Museum
Syracuse, New York

230

Robert Motherwell

**b. 1915, Aberdeen, Washington
active in Provincetown, 1959–present**

"Beside the Sea, With Sea Wave," 1968

oil on paper   29" × 22"

Collection of the artist
Greenwich, Connecticut

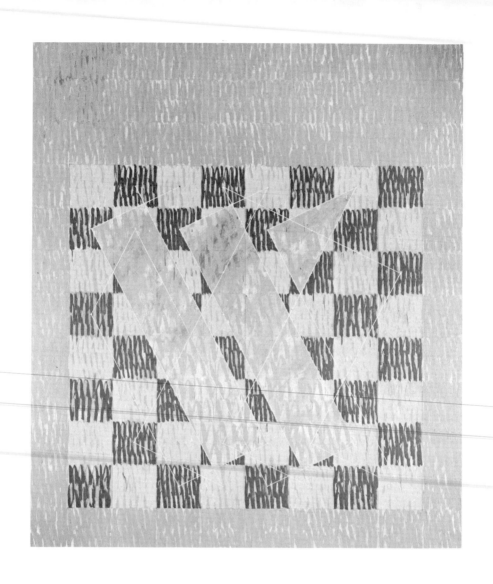

Jack Tworkov
b. 1900, Biala, Poland
active in Provincetown, 1923–35, 1954–present
"Knight Series OC #2 (Q3-75-#3), 1975
oil on canvas   90″ × 75″
Collection of Nancy Hoffman Gallery
New York, New York

232

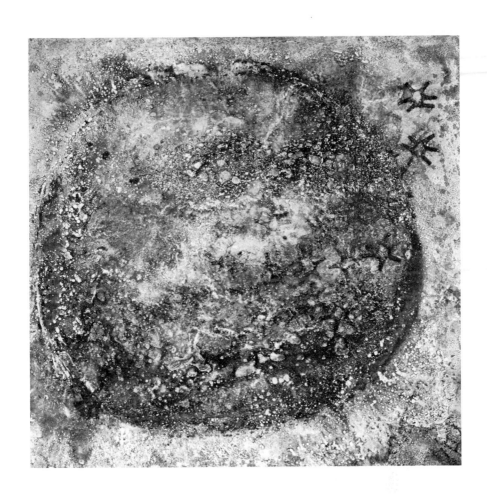

Yeffe Kimball
b. 1914, Mountain Park, Oklahoma
active in Provincetown, 1957–1974

"Copernicus," 1964

acrylic on canvas   5′ × 5′

Collection of the artist
New York, New York

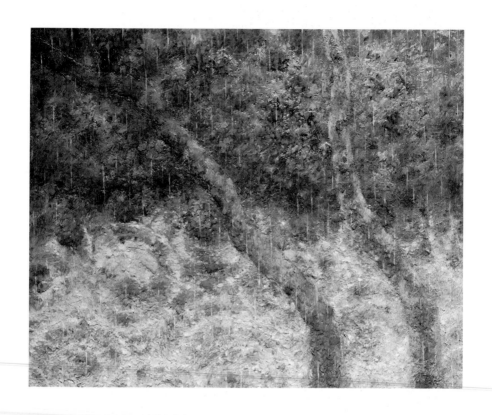

Sideo Fromboluti

b. 1920, Hershey, Pennsylvania
active in Provincetown 1950–present

"Rain on Patience Brook" 1976

oil on canvas   50″ × 60″

Collection of the Landmark Gallery
New York, New York

234

Earle Montrose Pilgrim
b. 1923, New York, New York   d. 1976
active in Provincetown, 1951–57

"Self-portrait," 1952

oil on canvas   12" × 18½"

Collection of Mrs. Earle Montrose Pilgrim
New York, New York

Gandy Brodie
b. 1924 d. 1975
"Sailboats Shadow" 1965
oil on board   9″ × 17¼″
Collection of Ronald A. Kuchta
Syracuse, New York

236

Jan Müller
b. 1922, Hamburg, Germany   d. 1958
active in Provincetown, 1955–1958

"Faust Scene with Red Mouse" 1956

oil on wood   11¼″ × 15¾″

Collection of Mr. and Mrs. Howard Wise
New York, New York

237

Jan Müller
b. 1922, Hamburg, Germany   d. 1958
active in Provincetown, 1955–1958

"The Witches," 1957

oil on wood shingle   9¼″ × 9¼″

Collection of the Gruenebaum Gallery
New York, New York

238

Lester Johnson
b. 1919, Minneapolis, Minnesota
active in Provincetown, 1953–1962

"Portrait with Feet #2," 1963

oil on canvas   72″ × 48″
Collection of Martha Jackson Gallery
New York, New York

Robert Beauchamp
b. 1923, Denver, Colorado
active in Provincetown, late 1950's and 1960's

Untitled 1965

oil on canvas   42″ × 42″

Collection of the artist
New York, New York

240

Bob Thompson

b. 1937, Louisville, Kentucky d. 1966
active in Provincetown, 1958–59, 1965

"The Spinning, Spinning, Turning, Directing"
1963

oil on canvas   63″ × 86½″

Collection of Martha Jackson Gallery
New York, New York

Warren Brandt
b. 1918, Ottensboro, North Carolina
active in Provincetown, 1960

"The Bride," 1963

oil on canvas   47″ × 58″

Collection of the Fishbach Gallery
New York, New York

242

Mervin Jules
b. 1912, Baltimore, Maryland
active in Provincetown, 1940, 1945–present

"Diner," 1975

oil on canvas   36″ × 45″

Collection of the A.C.A. Gallery
New York, New York

Irving Marantz

b. 1912, Elizabeth, New Jersey   d. 1973
active in Provincetown, 1947–1972

"Moonlight and Lovers," 1960

acrylic on canvas   50″ × 38″

Collection of Babcock Galleries
New York, New York

244

Wolf Kahn

b. 1927, Stuttgart, Germany
active in Provincetown, 1948, 1953–54, 1956

"Cabin Behind Herman Tasha's" 1953

oil on canvas   20″ × 26″

Collection of Grace Borgenicht Gallery
New York, New York

Nanno De Groot

b. 1913, Balbrug, Holland   d. 1963
active in Provincetown, 1948–1963

"Beach and Water," 1960

oil on canvas   52″ × 70″

Collection of Patricia De Groot
Provincetown, Massachusetts

246

Tony Vevers
b. 1926, London, England
Active in Provincetown 1955–present

"*Dawn*" 1966–1967

oil on canvas   38" × 31"

Collection of Babcock Gallery
New York, New York

Marcia Marcus
b. 1928, New York, New York
active in Provincetown, 1952–present

"Self Portrait with Poseidon," 1973

oil on canvas   42″ × 73″

Museum Purchase
Collection of Everson Museum
Syracuse, New York

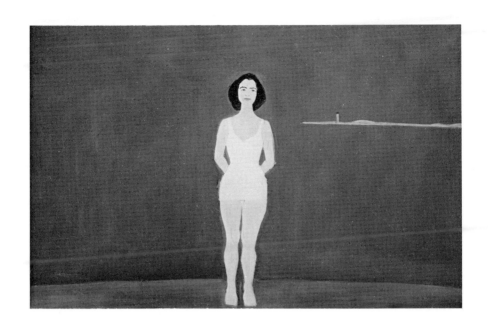

Alex Katz
b. 1927, New York, New York
active in Provincetown, 1958–1959

"Bather," 1959

oil on canvas 48″ × 72″

Collection of the artist
New York, New York

Martin Friedman

b. 1896, Budapest, Hungary
active in Provincetown 1955–present

"Golden Days"

oil on canvas   35″ × 45″

Collection of Babcock Galleries
New York, New York

250

Edward Giobbi
b. 1926, Waterbury, Connecticut
active in Provincetown late 1950's and 1960's

"Summer Provincetown, No. 10" 1975

watercolor   25″ × 32″

Collection of the artist
Katonah, New York

Herman Maril
b. 1908, Baltimore, Maryland
active in Provincetown, 1946–present

'Great Beach," 1966

40" × 60"

Collection of the artist
Baltimore, Maryland

Benny Andrews
b. 1930, Madison, Georgia
active in Provincetown, 1960

oil and collage   38″ × 24″

Collection of A.C.A. Galleries
New York, New York

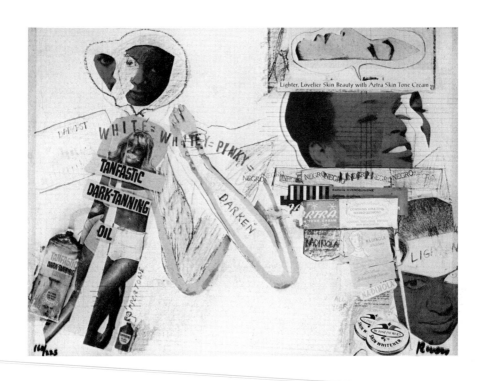

Larry Rivers

b. 1923, New York, New York
active in Provincetown, 1948–early 1960's

"Montage"

collage   23″ × 18″

Collection of Mr. Lawrence Richmond
Great Neck, New York

254

Taro Yamamoto

b. 1919, Hollywood, California
active in Provincetown 1951–present

"40 Commercial" 1969

oil on canvas   14″ × 19½″

Collection of Mr. Lawrence Richmond
Great Neck, New York

Mimi Gross

b. 1940, Manhattan, New York
active in Provincetown, 1943–present

"Six Figures"

pastel on paper   46″ × 35″

Collection of Mr. Lawrence Richmond
Great Neck, New York

(Mimi Gross and Red Grooms in foreground Chaim Gross and Lawrence
Richmond in center)

Red Grooms

b. 1937, Nashville, Tennessee
active in Provincetown 1959–1959

"Tappy Toes Theater" 1969

construction   27" × 28"

Collection of Mr. Lawrence Richmond
Great Neck, New York

257

Judith Rothschild

**b. 1922, New York, New York
active in Provincetown, 1949–present**

"Bathers III" 1976

oil on relief board   40″ × 60″

Collection of Lee Ault & Co., Inc.
New York, New York

Lila Katzen
b. 1932, Brooklyn, New York
active in Provincetown, 1949, 1956, 1958

"Diuturnal," 1964

acrylic on linen   52" × 85"

Collection of Phillip Katzen, Gloria Cortella Gallery
New York, New York

Edward Corbett
b. 1919, Chicago, Illinois   d. 1971
oil on canvas
active in Provincetown 1956–1971

"Provincetown 1969 IV," 1969

oil on canvas   40" × 30"

Collection of Borgenicht Gallery
New York, New York

260

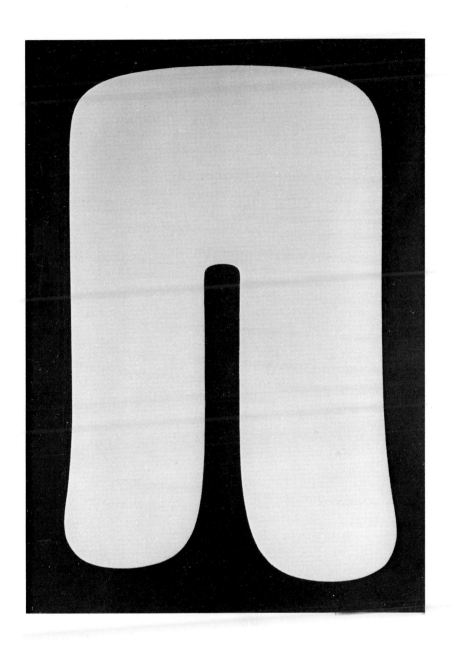

Myron Stout
b. 1908, Denton, Texas
active in Provincetown 1938, 1946–present

"No. 3 1957"

oil on canvas   26" × 18"

Collection of The Museum of Art, Carnegie Institute
Pittsburgh, Pennsylvania

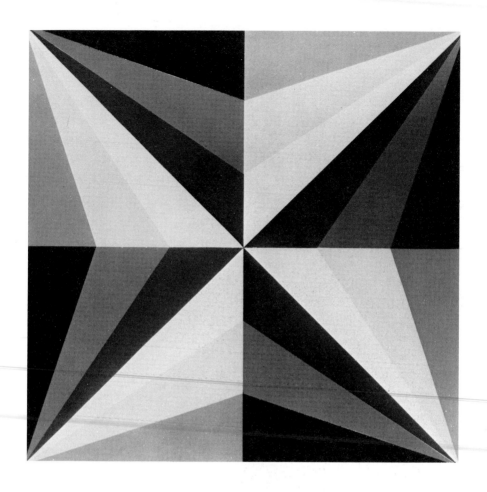

Nassos Daphnis
b. 1914, Krockeal, Greece
active in Provincetown, 1953–present

"#101–71." 1971

epoxy on canvas   6' × 6'

Collection of the artist
New York, New York

262

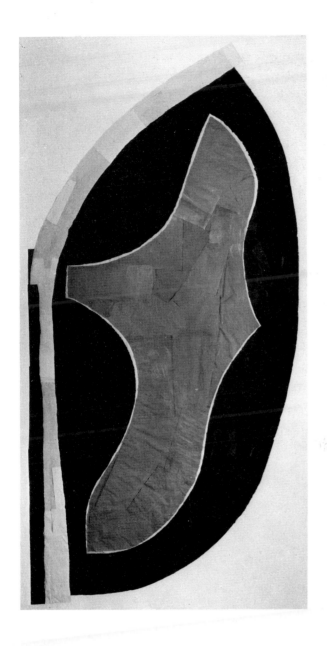

Fritz Bultman
b. 1919, New Orleans, Louisiana
active in Provincetown, 1938–present

"In the Sky Egg," 1973

mixed media on paper   96″ × 48″

Collection of Martha Jackson Gallery
New York, New York

Budd Hopkins
b. 1931, Wheeling, West Virginia
active in Provincetown, 1956–present
"City Life – for Donald Barthelme," 1974
oil on canvas   41″ × 43″
Collection of the Longpoint Gallery

264

Jo Anne Schneider
b. 1919, Lima, Ohio
"Double Boiler" 1975
oil on canvas   38″ × 46″
Collection of Jo Anne Schneider
New York, New York

Xavier Gonzalez
b. 1898, Almeria, Spain
active in Provincetown 1947–present

"Wellfleet Studio" 1970

oil on canvas   25" × 32"

Collection of the artist
New York, New York

266

Arthur Cohen
b. 1928, New York, N.Y.
active in Provincetown, 1961–present

"Provincetown," 1976
oil on canvas   27¾" × 48"

Collection of the artist
New York, New York

Alvin Ross

b. 1920, Vineland, New Jersey   d. 1975
active in Provincetown, 1950–1975

"From Woodstock to Provincetown" 1970

oil on canvas   50″ × 36″

Collection of Lenore Ross
Provincetown, Massachusetts

Jochen Seidel
b. 1924, Bitterfield, Germany   d. 1971
active in Provincetown, 1964–1971

"Am I Still Playing with the Mirror?"

ink and charcoal on paper   29″ × 23″

Collection of Martha Jackson Gallery
New York, New York

Peter Hutchinson
b. 1930, London, England
active in Provincetown, 1962–present
"K," 1974
From *The Alphabet Series*
color photgraphy, handwriting, mixed media   30″ × 40″
Collection of the John Gibson Gallery
New York, New York

BIBLIOGRAPHY

BOOKS

Ashton, Dore. *The New York School, a Cultural Reckoning.* New York: Viking Press, 1971.

Berger, Joseph. *(Jeremiah Digges): Cape Cod Pilot.* American Guide Series. New York: Viking Press, 1937. editorial and research assistance of the Federal Writers' Project, Works Progress Administration for the state of Massachusetts. reprint ed., Cambridge: The M.I.T. Press, 1969.

Brigadier, Anne. *Collage, a Complete Guide for Artists.* New York: Watson-Guptill Publications, Inc., 1970.

Canaday, John. *Mainstreams of Modern Art.* New York: Simon and Schuster, Inc., 1959.

Crotty, Frank. *Provincetown Profiles and others on Cape Cod.* Barre Gazetze, 1958.

Farnham, Emily. *Charles Demuth; behind a laughing mask.* Norman: University of Oklahoma Press, 1971.

Freeman, Richard B. *Niles Spencer.* Lexington: University of Kentucky Press, 1965.

Gloucester 350th Anniversary Celebration, Inc., ed. *Portrait of a Place, some American Landscape Painters in Gloucester.* Rockport: Nelson B. Robinson, 1973.

Goodrich, Lloyd. *Edward Hopper, 1882-1967.* New York: N. H. Abrams, 1971.

_____. *The Drawings of Edwin Dickinson.* New Haven: Yale University Press, 1963.

Havens, George R. *Frederick J. Waugh, American Maritime Painter.* Orono: University of Maine Press, 1969.

Hawthorne, Mrs. Charles W. ed. *Hawthorne on Painting.* New York: Dover Publications, Inc., 1960.

Jennings, Herman A. *Provincetown, or Odds and Ends from the Tip End.* Yarmouthport, 1890. facsimile ed., Provincetown: Peaked Hill Press, 1975.

Larkin, Oliver. *Art and Life in America.* New York: Holt, Rinehart, and Winston, Inc., 1949.

Luhan, Mabel Dodge. *Intimate Memories.* Vol. 3: *Movers and Shakers.* New York: Harcourt, Brace, and Company, Inc., 1936.

McCausland, Elizabeth. *Marsden Hartley.* Minneapolis: University of Minnestoa Press, 1952.

Miller, Dorothy C. ed. *Fifteen Americans.* New York: Museum of Modern Art, 1952.

Moffett, Ross. *Art in Narrow Streets, The First Thirty-three Years of the Provincetown Art Association, 1914-1947.* Falmouth: Kendall Printing Company, 1964.

Moritz, Charles, ed. *Current Biography Yearbook 1961.* New York: H. W. Wilson Company, 1961.

Novak, Barbara. *American Painting in the Nineteenth Century; Realism, Idealism, and the American Experience.* New York: Frederick A. Praeger Publishers, 1969.

O'Gorman, James F. *This other Gloucester.* Boston: 1976.

O'Gorman, James F. *Portrait of a Place: Some American Landscape Painters* of Gloucester (ex. cat.), Gloucester, Mass. 1973 (essay by John Wilmerding).

Parry, Albert. *Garrets and Pretenders, a History of Bohemianism in America.* revised ed., New York: Dover Publications, Inc., 1960.

Rewald, John. *Post-Impressionism from Van Gogh to Gauguin.* New York: Museum of Modern Art, 1956.

Rose, Barbara. *American Art Since 1900.* New York: Frederick A. Praeger Publishers, 1967.

_____. *Frankenthaler.* New York: H. N. Abrams, Inc., 1971.

Smith, Nancy W. Paine. *Provincetown Book.* Brockton: Tolman Print, Inc., 1922.

Soby, James Thrall. *Contemporary Painters.* New York: Museum of Modern Art, 1948.

Thoreau, Henry David. *Cape Cod.* Boston: Thicknor and Fields, 1865.

Travers, Milton A. *The Wampanoag Indian Federation of the Algonquin Nation.* New Bedford: Reynolds De Walt, 1957.

Vorse, Mary Heaton. *Time and the Town, a Provincetown Chronicle.* New York: The Dial Press, 1942.

Vuilleumier, Marion. *Indians of Old Cape Cod.* Taunton: William Sullwold, 1970.

Weeks, Sara T. and Hayes, Jr., Bartlett, ed. *Search for the Real.* Cambridge: The M.I.T. Press, 1948.

Young, Mahonri Sharp. *Early American Moderns (Painters of the Stieglitz Group).* New York: Watson-Guptill Publications, Inc., 1974.

One Hundred Years of Growing with Provincetown. Provincetown: The First National Bank, 1954.

Provincetown Guidebook. Provincetown: Provincetown Art Association, 1928.

CATALOGS

The American Federation of Arts, New York.
Milton Avery; 1960
Monograph with essay by Adelyn Breeskin.

The American Federation of Arts, New York.
Lee Gatch; 1960.
Exhibition catalog with essay by Perry T. Rathbone.

The Amon Carter Museum of Western Art, Fort Worth, Texas.
Taos and Santa Fe; the artist's environment 1882–1942; 1963.
Exhibition catalog by Van Deren Coke.

Babcock Galleries, New York.
E. Ambrose Webster 1869–1935; November 2 to November 27, 1965.
Exhibition catalog with essay by Vivien Raynor.

Baltimore Museum of Art, Baltimore, Maryland.
Herman Maril; 1967.
Monograph with introduction by Frank Getlein.

The Brooklyn Museum, Brooklyn, New York.
William Zorbach/Paintings, watercolors, and drawings 1911–1922; November 26, 1968 to January 19, 1969.
Exhibition catalog by Donelson F. Hoopes.

Chapellier Gallery, New York.
George Elmer Browne 1871–1946; November 1968.
Exhibition catalog with essay by George Albert Perret.

The Chrysler Museum of Art, Provincetown, Massachusetts.
Hawthorne Retrospective; June 16 to September 17, 1961.
Exhibiton catalog with introduction by E. P. Richardson; appreciation by Hans Hofmann; foreword by Jo Hawthorne.

The Chrysler Museum of Art, Provincetown, Massachusetts, Provincetown Arts Festival.

272

American Art of our Time; 1958.
Exhibition catalog with foreword by
Harris K. Prior.

Everson Museum of Art, Syracuse,
New York.
The Valley of Kathmandu/Leo Manso;
April 9 to May 23, 1976.
Exhibition catalog with introduction by
Gordon Brown.

John Gibson Gallery, New York.
Alphabet Series/Peter Hutchinson;
summer 1974.
Exhibition catalog.

Guild Hall, Easthampton, New York.
Artists and Easthampton, a
bicentennial exhibition; August 14 to
October 3, 1976.
Exhibition catalog.

International Exhibitions Foundations,
Washington, D.C.
Karl Knaths, five decades of painting;
1973–1974.
Exhibition catalog with introduction by
Charles Edward Eaton

Joe and Emily Lowe Art Gallery,
Syracuse University, Syracuse, New
York.
Botkin '72; March 13 to April 1, 1972.
Exhibition catalog.

Marlborough Galleries, New York.
Adolph Gottlieb/Paintings 1971–1972;
November 1972.
Exhibition catalog.

Museum of Modern Art, New York.
Feininger/Hartley; 1944.
Monograph.

Museum of Modern Art, New York.
Jackson Pollock; 1967.
Exhibition catalog with extended
chronology by Francis V. O'Connor.

Museum of Modern Art, New York.
The New American Painting, as shown
in southern European countries;
1958–1959.
Exhibition catalog.

National Academy of Design, New
York.
A Century and a Half of American Art
1825–1975; October 10 to November
16, 1975.
Exhibition catalog.

National Collection of Fine Arts,
Smithsonian Institution, Washington,
D.C.
Milton Avery; December 12, 1969 to
January 25, 1970.
Exhibition catalog with introduction by
Adelyn D. Breeskin.

National Collection of Fine Arts,
Smithsonian Institution, Washington,
D.C.
Marguerite Zorach: The Early Years,
1908–1920; December 7, 1973 to
February 3, 1974.
Exhibition catalog.

The Phillips Gallery, Washington, D.C.
Karl Knaths; 1957.
Exhibition catalog with introduction by
Duncan Phillips; appreciation by
Emanuel Benson; commentary by Karl
Knaths.

Poindexter Gallery, New York.
Budd Hopkins/Master of Movement
Manque; February 22 to March 12,
1966.
Exhibition catalog.

Provincetown Art Association,
Provincetown, Massachusetts.
Edwin Dickinson; August 14 to
September 7, 1976.
Exhibition catalog.

Provincetown Art Association,
Provincetown, Massachusetts.
Golden Anniversary Exhibition; August
2 to October 6, 1964.
Exhibition catalog.

Provincetown Art Association,
Provincetown, Massachusetts.
Charles Hawthorne; July 4 to
September 7, 1952.
Exhibition catalog with appreciation by
Hans Hofmann.

San Francisco Museum of Art, San
Francisco, California.

Edward Corbett; March 28 to May 4, 1969.
Exhibition catalog with essay by Gerald Nordland.

Smith College Museum of Art, Northampton, Massachusetts.
An Exhibition of the Work of Robert Motherwell; January 10 to January 28, 1963.
Exhibition catalog with interview by Margaret Paul.

Solomon R. Guggenheim Museum, New York.
Jan Müller 1922–58; January 11 to February 25, 1962.
Exhibition catalog.

University of California Art Gallery, Santa Barbara, California.
Charles Demuth/the mechanical encrusted on the living; October 5 to November 14, 1971.
Exhibition catalog.

University of Connecticut, Storrs, Connecticut.
The Paintings of Charles Hawthorne; October 12 to November 7, 1968.
Exhibition catalog with introduction by Marvin S. Sadik.

University Art Museum, University of Texas, Austin, Texas.
Marsden Hartley; Painter/Poet, 1877–1943; January 10 to February 16, 1969.
Exhibition catalog.

Vassar College Art Gallery, Poughkeepsie, New York.
Woodstock/an American art colony 1902–1977; January 23 to March 4, 1977.
Exhibition catalog.

Vose Galleries of Boston, Inc., Boston, Massachusetts.
Gerrit A. Beneker (1882–1934)/painter of American industry; 1976.
Exhibition catalog.

Whitney Museum of American Art, New York.
Edwin Dickinson; 1966.
Exhibition catalog.

Whitney Museum of American Art, New York.
Franz Kline 1910–1962; November 1968.
Exhibition catalog.

Worcester Art Museum, Worcester, Massachusetts.
Ross Moffett 1888–1971; May 30 to July 6, 1975.
Exhibition catalog.

PERIODICALS

Bell, John D. "A 350 Year Voyage to Hell." *Provincetown Art Association Catalogue and Guidebook.*

Brunelle, Al. "Nassos Daphnis: Obsession with the Harvest." *Art News* 72 (April 1973) 75–6.

de Kooning, Elaine. "Dickinson and Kiesler." *Art News* 51 (April 1952) 20–3.

Goldwater, Robert. "Reflections on the Rothko Exhibition." *Art Magazine* 35 (March 1961) 42–5.

Phillips, Duncan. "Lee Gatch." *Magazine of Art* 42 (December 1949) 282–7.

Seckler, Dorothy Gees. "Can Painting be Taught?" *Art News* 50 (March 1951) 40+.

Seckler, Dorothy Gees. "Adolph Gottlieb Makes a Facade." *Art News* 54 (March 1955) 42–5+.

Seckler, Dorothy Gees. "Lee Gatch." *Art in America* 44 (Fall 1956) 28–32.

Seckler, Dorothy Gees. "Notes on Work in Progress from Woodstock, New York." *Archives of American Art Journal* October 1963.

Horizon. New York: American Heritage Publishing Company 3 (July 1961) no. 6.

"Easthampton." *Lippincott's Magazine,* 1883.

Santa Barbara Museum of Art. *Bulletin, 1969.* 1 (January 1970) no. 1.

Sarasota Art Association, Sarasota, Florida. release on Helen Sawyer, April 11, 1971.

NEWSPAPERS

Cape Cod Compass
Cape Cod Standard Times. News features, June 23, 1949; July 5, 1949; August 13, 1949.

"Art Pioneers to be Honored." *Cape Cod Standard Times,* June 30, 1949.

New York Times. Obituary, February 26, 1970.

"Witherstine to Open Central Gallery for Fine Arts and Discussion Here." *Provincetown Advocate,* June 23, 1949.

"What is an Artist?" *Provincetown Advocate,* June 30, 1949.

de Kooning, Elaine. "Record Exhibit of Abstract Painters Shown at Cape End." *Provincetown Advocate,* July 5, 1949.

Browne, Rosalind. "Art World Eyes Forum '49 Program of Abstract Work and Discussions." *Provincetown Advocate,* July 7, 1949.

"Real Jazz is Hot Forum '49 Topic." *Provincetown Advocate,* July 14, 1949.

Provincetown Advocate, August 4, 1949.

"Architectural Trends to be Charted." *Provincetown Advocate,* August 11, 1949.

"Forum '49 Spotlights Early Pioneers in Modern Movement in American Art." *Provincetown Advocate,* summer 1949.

Provincetown Advocate, November 3, 1966.

Kingsley, April. "The Tirca-Karlis Gallery." *Provincetown Advocate.* Summer Guide, August 1, 1974.

"Tirca Karlis Cohen." *Provincetown Advocate.* Obituary, November 21, 1974.

Sheridan, Lee. "Art Alive in Provincetown." *Springfield Daily News,* August 15, 1974.

LETTERS

Benny Andrews to the writer, summer and fall 1976
Peter Busa to the writer
Nassos Daphnis to the writer, fall 1976
Josephine Del Deo to the writer, February 1977
Lila Katzen to the writer, May 1976
Welden Kees to Adolph Gottlieb (lent by Esther Gottlieb)
Stuart Preston to Welden Kees, summer 1949
Helen Sawyer to the writer, August and September 1976
Judith Shahn to the writer, November 1975
Jack Tworkov to the writer, summer 1975

RECORDINGS

Bultman, Fritz. Transcript of a talk on Hans and "Miz" Hofmann at the Smithsonian Institution, Washington, D.C., fall 1976.

"Pop Art Symposium." Provincetown Art Association, summer 1963.

WRITER'S TAPED INTERVIEWS FOR ARCHIVES OF AMERICAN ART

Arnold Blanch, 1963
Paul Burlin, 1962
Peter Busa, 1965
Walter P. Chrysler, Jr., 1964
Nassos Daphnis, 1964
Edwin Dickinson, 1962
Perle Fine, 1968
Richard Florsheim, 1968
Adolph Gottlieb, 1967
John Grillo, 1964
Red Grooms, 1965
Nathan Halper, 1963
Budd Hopkins, 1965
Lila Katzen, 1964
Karl Knaths, 1962
Sam Kootz, 1964
George McNeil, 1965
Philip Malicoat, 1965
Leo Manso, 1965
Herman Maril, 1965
Ross Moffett, 1962
Myron Stout, 1965
Jack Tworkov, 1962
Tony Vevers, 1965

WRITER'S TAPED INTERVIEWS

Elise Asher, summer 1976
Fritz Bultman, spring 1976
William Freed, summer 1976
Miz Hofmann, 1962
Boris Margo, 1960's
Lillian Orlowsky, summer 1976
Judith Rothschild, spring 1976
Sol Wilson, summer 1968

OTHER INTERVIEWS

Taped interview with Red Grooms by Paul Cummings for Archives of American Art, 1965.

Interview with Helen Sawyer by Earnest W. Watson.

CONVERSATIONS WITH THE WRITER

Benny Andrews, summer 1976
Carl Ashby, summer 1976
Milton Avery, summers 1957 and 1959
Sally Michel Avery, fall 1975
Helen Avlon, summer 1976
Will Barnet, winter 1977
Ethel Baziotes, winter 1975
Maurice Berezov, winter 1976
Henry Botkin, summers 1975 and 1976
Warren Brandt, 1958, 1959, and winter 1977
Ann Brigadier, winter 1977
Byron Browne, late 1950's
Fritz Bultman, summer 1975 and winter 1976
Paul Burlin, summers late 1950's
Katherine Burnside, summer 1975
Peter Busa, winter 1977
Reggie Cabral, summer 1976
Georgio Cavallon, 1960's to summer 1976
Mr. Clancey (Rehn's Gallery), spring 1976
Nassos Daphnis, 1957 to 1976
Edwin Dickinson, summer 1968
Ray Donarsky, winter 1976
Reeves Euler, summer 1976
Perle Fine, winter 1976
Richard Florsheim, 1977
Jim Forsberg, summers 1975 and 1976
Elsie Driggs Gatch, winter 1976
Edward Giobbi, winter 1977
Adolph Gottlieb, summer 1965
Esther Gottlieb, summer 1965 and winter 1977
John Grillo, winter 1977
Sidney Gross, summers late 1950's
Raoul Hague, summer 1963
Nathan Halper, summers 1975 and 1976, winters 1976 and 1977
Jo Hawthorne, summer 1976
Henry Hensche, fall 1975 and summer 1976
Hans Hofmann, 1959 to 1963
Miz Hofmann, summers 1959 to 1963
Budd Hopkins, fall 1976
Marit Jensen, summer 1976
Wolf Kahn, fall 1975
Martha Kantor, fall 1976
Alex Katz, spring 1976

Franz Kline, 1957 and 1958
Stewart Klonis, summer 1963
Sam Kootz, winters 1976 and 1977
Karl Knaths, summers 1963 to 1972
Lee Krasner, spring 1976
Toni Lasell, late 1960's to summer 1976
Esther Locke, summer 1976
Bruce McKain, fall 1975 and summer 1976
George McNeil, winter 1976
Philip Malicoat, summers 1975 and 1976
Arnie Manos, summers 1975 and 1976
Marilyn Manos, summers 1975 and 1976
Leo Manso, fall 1976
Marcia Marcus, summer 1975
Boris Margo, summer 1976
Dody James Müller, winter 1975
Steve Pace, late 1950's and winters 1976 and 1977
Ian Pinkerton, summer 1976
Ann Poor, fall 1976
Peter Poor, fall 1976
Paul Resik, winter 1976
Mark Rothko, summer 1969
Judith Rothschild, winter, spring, and summer 1976
Therese Schwartz, summer 1953, spring 1976, winter 1977
Raphael Soyer, fall 1975
Myron Stout, summers 1975 and 1976
Jack Tworkov, summers 1975 and 1976
Elspeth Vevers, summers 1975 and 1976
Tony Vevers, summers 1975 and 1976
Murray Wax, summers 1975 and 1976
Peter Whitehead, summer 1963
Marjorie Windust, summer 1976
George Yater, summer 1975
Virginia Zabriskie, fall 1976

MISCELLANEOUS

Fine Arts Work Center, Provincetown, Massachusetts. Brochures.

Hofmann, Hans and Bultman, Fritz. "Protest Against Ostrich Attitudes in the Arts." (Hand typed manifesto, lent by Esther Gottlieb)

Hirschl and Adler Gallery, New York. Photgraph files, notes and data on works.

Lists compiled by Nathan Halper.

New York Public Library, New York. Fine Arts Division, artists files.

Provincetown Art Association, Provincetown, Massachusetts. Collection, files.

APPENDIX

A List of Painters Who Have Painted in Provincetown — (Date & place of birth, date of death and date of activity in Provincetown)

Nicolas Afonchikov (Afon)
b. 1888, Taganrog, U.S.S.R.   d. 1976
1936–1976

Maud Ainslie
b. 1871, Louisville, Kentucky   d. 1960
1916–1950

Courtney Allen
b. 1895, Norfolk, Virginia   d. 1969
1919–1969

Erma Paul Allen
b. 1877, Washington, D.C.
1921–present

Mary Cecil Allen
b. 1893, Australia   d. 1960's
1950's, 1960's

Benny Andrews
b. 1930, Madison, Georgia
1960

Carl Ashby
b. 1914, San Rita, New Mexico
1940's

Elise Asher
b. 1914, Chicago, Illinois
1950–present

William Auerbach-Levy
b. 1889, Brest-Litovsk, U.S.S.R.
1921–1925

George Ault
b. 1891, Cleveland, Ohio   d. 1948
1922–1927

Edward Avedesian
b. 1936, Lowell, Massachusetts
1962

Milton Avery
b. 1893, Altmar, New York   d. 1965
1956, 1960

Salley Avery
b. ?, Brooklyn, New York
1956–1960

Peggy Bacon
b. 1895, Ridgefield, Connecticut
1915–1917, 1945

LaForce Bailey
b. 1893, Joliet, Illinois
1928, 1935, 1947, 1959

Robert E. Ball
b. 1890, Kansas City, Missouri   d. late 1930's
1925, 1936, 1937

Will Barnet
b. 1911, Beverly, Massachusetts
1957–1958

Bill Barrell
b. 1932, London, England
1957–1961

Wallace Bassford
b. ?, St. Louis, Missouri
1936, 1937, 1945–47, 1956–present

Mark Baum
b. 1903, Sanok, Poland
1932, 1936–37, 1956

William Baziotes
b. 1912, Pittsburgh, Pennsylvania
d. 1963
1946–1950

Gifford Beal
b. 1879, New York, New York   d. 1956
1916, 1921, 1922

Reynolds Beal
b. 1867, New York, New York   d. 1951
1900–1919

Robert Beauchamp
b. 1923, Denver, Colorado
late 1950's and 1960's

Hazel Belvo
b. 1934, Dayton, Ohio
1960–present

Gerrit Beneker
b. 1882, Grand Rapids, Michigan
d. 1934
1915–1934

Maurice Berezov
b. ?, Paris, France
1929–1933

Janice Biala
b. 1904, Biala, Poland
1923–1928

William Harry Warren Bicknell
b. 1860, Boston, Massachusetts
d. 1943
1918–1943

George Biddle
b. 1885, Philadelphia, Pennsylvania
d. 1973
1946–1973

Al Bing
b. 1878, New York, New York   d. 1959
1956–1958

Nell Blaine
b. 1922, Richmond, Virginia
1943, 1948, 1949

Varujan Boghosian
b. 1925, New Britain, Connecticut
1947–present

Max Bohm
b. 1868, Cleveland, Ohio   d. 1923
1916–1923

Cameron Booth
b. 1892, Erie, Pennsylvania
1920's

Helen Boswell
b. 1906, Chicago, Illinois   d. 1969
1934–late 1960's

Henry Botkin
b. 1896, Boston, Massachusetts
1950–present

Warren Brandt
b. 1918, Ottensboro, North Carolina
1960

Anne Brigadier
b. 1908, New York, New York
1940–present

Gandy Brodie
b. 1924, New York, New York   d. 1975
1947–early 1960's

Byron Browne
b. 1907, Yonkers, New York
d. 1961
1952–1961

George Elmer Browne
b. 1871, Gloucester, Massachusetts
d. 1946
1919–1948

Lodewijk Bruckman
b. 1913, LeHague, Holland
1953–early 1960's

Edith Bry
b. 1898, St. Louis, Missouri

Fritz Bultman
b. 1919, New Orleans, Louisiana
1938–present

Paul Burlin
b. 1886, New York, New York   d. 1969
early 1930's, late 1950's, late 1960's

Katherine Burnside
b. ?, Ft. Worth, Texas
1950–present

Peter Busa
b. 1914, Pittsburgh, Pennsylvania
1936–1970

Lawrence Calcagno
b. 1913, San Francisco, Cal.
1950's

Elizabeth Howland Caliga
b. ?   d. c. 1960
1916–1950

Isaac Howland Caliga
b. 1857, Auburn, Indiana   d. c.1940
1936

Jaques Joseph Camius
b. 1904, Odessa, U.S.S.R.
1959–present

Victor Candell
b. 1903, Budapest, Hungary   d. 1977
1956–1976

Norman Carton
b. 1908, U.S.S.R.
1959–1965

Giorgio Cavallon
b. 1904, Sorlo, Italy
1927–present

Oliver Newberry Chaffee
b. 1881, Detroit, Michigan   d. 1944
1913–1944

Francis Chapin
b. 1899, Bristol, Ohio   d. 1965
1933–1940

Carmen L. Cicero
b. Chicago, Illinois
information unavailable

James Floyd Clymer
b. 1893, Perkosie, Pennsylvania
1916, 1922–1940

Ruth Cobb
b. 1914, Boston, Massachusetts
1947–1950's

Arthur Cohen
b. 1928, New York, New York
1961–present

Jean Cohen
b. 1927, New York, New York
1955–present

Lila Copeland
b. 1922, New York, New York
1957–1976

Charles Couper
b. 1924, Portsmouth, New Hampshire
1963–present

Edward Corbett
b. 1919, Chicago, Illinois   d. 1971
1956–1971

Edgar Corbridge
b. ?
1930–1960

Emilio Cruz
b. 1938, New York, New York
1957–1963

e. e. cummings
b. 1894, Cambridge, Massachusetts
d. 1962
1930

Nassos Daphnis
b. 1914, Krockeal, Greece
1953–present

Helen Daphnis-Avlon
b. 1932, New York, New York
1953–present

Morris Davidson
b. 1898, Rochester, New York
1925–present

Stuart Davis
b. 1894, Philadelphia, Pennsylvania
d. 1964
1913

Victor DeCarlo
b. 1916, New Haven, Connecticut
d. 1973
1946–1973

Peter Dechar
b. 1942, New York, New York
1964, 1965

Pat DeGroot
b. 1930, London, England
1948–present

Nanno De Groot
b. 1913, Balkbrug, Holland   d. 1963
1948–1963

Elaine DeKooning
b. 1920, New York, New York

Salvatore Del Deo
b. 1928, Providence, Rhode Island
1946–present

Charles Henry Demuth
b. 1873, Lancaster, Pennsylvania
d. 1935
1914, 1919–1920, 1930

Robert DeNiro
b. 1922, Syracuse, New York
1950's, 1971, 1973

Vivian DePinna
b. 1883
1948–1969

Frank Desch
b. 1873, Philadelphia, Pennsylvania
d. 1934
1916–1934

Edwin Walter Dickinson
b. 1891, Seneca Falls, New York
1912–present

Arthur Diehl
b. ?, England
1913

Joseph DiGiusto
b. 1901, Boston, Massachusetts
1950's–1960's

Al DiLauro
b. 1930, Philadelphia, Pennsylvania
1955–present

John Dos Passos
b. 1896, Chicago, Illinois   d. 1970
1915, 1930's–1946

William Draper
b. 1912, Hopedale, Massachusetts
1929–1936

Elsie Driggs
b. 1898, Hartford, Connecticut
1930

Florida Duncan
b. Ontario, Canada   d. 1932
1916

Ablert Edel
b. ?, France
1920's, 1930's

Ethel Edwards
b. ?, New Orleans, Louisiana
1947–present

Marisol (Escobar)
b. 1930, Paris, France
1950–1955

Edwin Reeves Euler
b. 1896, DeLamar, Nevada
1919–present

Jerry Farnsworth
b. 1895, Dalton, Georgia
1915–1972

Remo Farrugio
b. 1906, Palermo, Italy
1960–present

Perle Fine
b. 1906, Boston, Massachusetts
1938–1951

Richard Florsheim
b. 1916, Chicago, Illinois
1954–present

Jim Forsberg
b. 1919, Sauk Center, Minnesota
1953–present

John L. Frank
b. 1929, Chicago, Illinois
1954–present

Mary Frank
b. 1933, London, England
1963–1964

Helen Frankenthaler
b. 1928, New York, New York
1957–1969

John Robinson Frazier
b. 1889, Stonington, Connecticut
d. 1966
1913–1966

William Freed
b. 1902, Poland
1945–present

Martin Friedman
b. 1896, Budapest, Hungary
1955–present

Frederick Carl Frieseke
b. 1874, Owosso, Michigan   d. 1939
1921

Sideo Fromboluti
b. 1920, Hershey, Pennsylvania
1950–present

James Gahagan
b. 1927, New York, New York
1949, 1950, 1952–present

R. H. Ives Gammel
b. 1893, Providence, Rhode Island
1915–1968

Lee Gatch
b. 1902, Baltimore, Maryland   d. 1968
1930–1940's

Jan Gelb
b. 1906, New York, New York
1935–present

Oscar H. Gieberich
b. 1886, New York, New York
late teens–1940's

Ed Giobbi
b. 1926, Waterbury, Connecticut
late 1950's and 1960's

Leah Gold
b. 1912, New York, New York
1949–1976

Ann Goldthwaite
b. c. 1870, Montgomery, Alabama
d. 1944
1890's, 1938

Shirley Gorelick
b. 1924, Brooklyn, New York
1948–present

Adolph Gottlieb
b. 1903, New York, New York   d. 1974
1946–1958

Jack Gregory
b. 1938, Fall River, Massachusetts
late 60's–1973

John Grillo
b. 1917, Lawrence, Massachusetts
1949–present

Peter J. Grippe
b. 1912, Buffalo, New York
1938–present

Mimi Grooms
b. 1940, Manhattan, New York
1943–present

Red Grooms
b. 1937, Nashville, Tennessee
1957–1959

Chaim Gross
b. 1904, Kolomea, East Austria
1924, 1938, 1939, 1943–present

George Grosz
b. 1893, Berlin, Germany
d. 1959
1937–1945

Xavier Gonzalez
b. 1898, Almeria, Spain
1947–present

Lena Gurr
b. 1897, Brooklyn, New York
1955–present

Mary Hackett
b. 1906, New York, New York
1931–present

William Formby Halsall
b. 1841, Kirkdale, England   d. 1919
1890's–1919

Al Hanson
b. 1924, Osceola, Nebraska
1950's, mid-1960's

Lily Harmon
b. 1912, New Haven, Connecticut
1956–present

Marsden Hartley
b. 1877, Lewiston, Maine   d. 1943
1917

Frederick Childe Hassam
b. 1859, Dorchester, Massachusetts
d. 1935
1900–1901

Charles Webster Hawthorne
b. 1872, Richmond, Maine   d. 1930
1915–1930

Robert Hebert
b. 1939 Fall River, Massachusetts
1960's

William Hegelheimer
b. ?, Colorado   d. 1973
1960's

Charles Lloyd Heinz
b. 1885, Shelbyville, Illinois   d. 1953
1929–1953

Robert Henry
b. 1933, Brooklyn, New York
1952

Henry Hensche
b. 1901, Chicago, Illinois
1922–present

Hans O. Hofmann
b. 1880, Weissenberg, Bavaria
d. 1966
1932–1966

Gerrit Hondius
b. 1891, Kampen, Holland   d. 1970
1952–1970

Budd Hopkins
b. 1931, Wheeling, West Virginia
1956–present

Edward Hopper
b. 1882, Nyack, New York   d. 1967
1930–1967

Jo N. Hopper
b. ?
1930–1967

Peter Hunt
b. c. 1898, New York, New York
d. 1969
1930–1960

Robert Douglas Hunter
b. 1928, Boston, Massachusetts
1949–present

Peter Arthur Hutchinson
b. 1930, London, England
1962–present

Angelo Ippolito
b. 1922, St. Arsenio, Italy
1956–1965

Dody James
b. 1927, Dallas, Texas
1956–1959

Claud Jensen
b. ?, Sprague, Washington
1945–present

Marit Jensen
b. ?, Buffalo, New York
1945–present

Lester Johnson
b. 1919, Minneapolis, Minnesota
1953–1962

Stella Johnson
b.
1920–1950's

Mervin Jules
b. 1912, Baltimore, Maryland
1940, 1945–present

Charles Kaeselau
b. 1889, Stockholm, Sweden   d. 1970
1915–1941

Wolf Kahn
b. 1927, Stuttgart, Germany
1948, 1953–54, 1956

Howie Kanovitz
b. 1929, Fall River, Massachusetts
1953–present

Morris Kantor
b. 1896, Minsk, U.S.S.R.   d. 1974
1930's

Joe Kaplan
b. 1900, Minsk, U.S.S.R.
early 1920's–present

Alex Katz
b. 1927, New York, New York
1958–1959

Lila Katzen
b. 1932, Brooklyn, New York
1949, 1956, 1958–present

Julius Katzieff
b. 1892, Lithuania
1920–1960's

Weldon Kees
b. 1914, Beatrice, Nebraska   d. 1955
1949

Gyorgy Kepes
b. 1906, Sehip, Hungary
1945–present

Yeffe Kimball
b. 1914, Mountain Park, Oklahoma
1957–1974

Franz Kline
b. 1910, Wilkes-Barre, Pennsylvania
d. 1962
late 1950's–1962

Karl Knaths
b. 1891, EauClaire, Wisconsin
d. 1971
1919–1971

Lee Krasner
b. 1911, Brooklyn, New York
1938–1944

Leon Kroll
b. 1884, New York, New York   d. 1974

Thom Kuka
b. ?
1960's, early 1970's

Yasuo Kuniyoshi
b. 1893, Okayama, Japan   d. 1953
1940's

Sharli Powers Land
b. ?
late 1960's, early 1970's

Dorothy Antoinette LaSelle
b. c. 1902, Beatrice, Nebraska
1944–present

Ernest Lawson
b. 1873, Halifax, Nova Scotia   d. 1939
1920

Blanche Lazzell
b. ?, Maidsville, Virginia
d. 1956
1916–1956

Frank Lee
b. 1908
1950–late 1960's

Mary Letson
b. 1900, Grand Forks, North Dakota
d. 1971
1960's–1971

Lucy L'Engle
b. 1889, New York, New York
1911–present

William Johnson L'Engle
b. 1884, Jacksonville, Florida   d. 1957
1916–1957

Linda Lindeberg
b. 1915, New York, New York   d. 1973
1953–1973

Tod Lindenmuth
b. 1885, Allentown, Pennsylvania
1915–1940

Loren MacIver
b. 1909, New York, New York
1930–1938

Bruce McKain
b. 1900, Freetown, Indiana
1928–present

Mildred M. McMillan
b. 1884, Chicago, Illinois
1915, 1920's, 1930's

George McNeil
b. 1908, Brooklyn, New York
1935–1963

Phil Malicoat
b. 1908, Indianapolis, Indiana
1929–present

Leo Manso
b. 1914, New York, New York
1947–present

Irving Marantz
b. 1912, Elizabeth, New Jersey
d. 1973
1947–1972

Marcia Marcus
b. 1928, New York, New York
1952–present

Boris Margo
b. 1902, Wolotschisk, U.S.S.R.
1949–present

Herman Maril
b. 1908, Baltimore, Maryland
1946–present

Ethel Mars
b. 1876, Springfield, Illinois   d.
1915–1928

Charles E. Martin
b. 1910, Chelsea, Massachusetts
1927–1935

Alice Trumbull Mason
b. 1904, Litchfield, Connecticut
d. 1971
1927–1928

Emily Mason
b. 1932, New York, New York
1955

Eleanor Meldahl
b. 1928, Vancouver, Canada
1969–present

Lily Michael
b. ?, London, England
1956–present

Jay Milder
b. 1934, Omaha, Nebraska
1958–1962

Richard Emile Miller
b. 1875, St. Louis, Missouri   d. 1943
1915–1943

Frank Milby
b. 1933, New York, New York
1967, 1969–present

Ross E. Moffett
b. 1888, Clearfield, Iowa   d. 1971
1913–1971

George Morrison
b. 1919, Minnesota
1950–1968

Robert Motherwell
b. 1915, Aberdeen, Washington
1959–present

Seong Moy
b. 1921, Canton, China
1946, 1954–present

Jan Müller
b. 1922, Hamburg, Germany   d. 1958
1955–1958

May Murphy
b. ?   d. 1977
information unavailable

Barnett Newman
b. 1905, New York, New York   d. 1970
1950's

John Noble
b. 1874, Witchita, Kansas   d. 1934
1919–1934

Bror Julius Olsson Nordfeldt
b. 1878, Sweden   d. 1955
1916–early 1920's

Claes Thure Oldenburg
b. 1929, Stockholm, Sweden
1959

Samuel Edmund Oppenhiem
b. ?
1926–present

Lillian Orlowsky
b. 1914, New York, New York
1938, 1945–present

Elliot Orr
b. 1904, Flushing, New York
1926, 1945–present

Stephen Pace
b. 1918, Charleston, Missouri
1956–1966

Pauline Palmer
b. ?, McHenry, Ilinois   d. ?
1920's, 1930's

Walter Edward Parsons
b. 1890, Troy, Pennsylvania
late 1930's, 1953–1955

James Wingate Parr
b. 1923, Boston, Massachusetts
d. 1969
1948–1969

William McGregor Paxton
b. 1869, Boston, Massachusetts
d. 1941
1916–1940

Louise Pershing
b. 1904, Pittsburgh, Pennsylvania
late 1940's–present

Heinrich Pfeiffer
b. ?
1920–1944

Robert Philip
b. 1895, New York, New York
1938

Earle Montrose Pilgrim
b. 1923, New York, New York   d. 1976
1951–1957

Ian Pinkerson
b. 1913, Plymouth, Massachusetts
1945–present

Jackson Pollock
b. 1912, Cody, Wyoming   d. 1956
1943–1944

Henry Varnum Poor
b. 1888, Chapman, Kansas   d. 1970
1933–1970

Ethel Rabin
b. ?
1950–present

Vollian Burr Rann
b. 1897, Wilmington, North Carolina
d. 1956
1922–1956

Ellen Ravenscroft
b. 1885, Jackson, Mississippi
1918–1947

Ada Raynor
b. 1901, London, England
1930–present

Ruth Reeves
b. 1892, Redlands, California
early 1950's

Anton Refregier
b. 1905, Moscow, U.S.S.R.
1931

Paul Resika
b. 1928, New York, New York
1947, 1964–present

Robert Richenberg
b. 1917, Boston, Massachusetts
1946–present

Helen Richter
(Information not obtainable)

Mischa Richter
(Information not obtainable)

Larry Rivers
b. 1923, New York, New York
1948–early 1960's

Romanos Rizk
b. 1927, Providence, Rhode Island
1949–present

Jo Roman
b. 1917, Cambridge, Massachusetts
1962, 1963, 1965

Mel Roman
b. 1927, New York, New York
1962, 1963, 1972, 1974, 1975

Umberto Romano
b. 1906, Naples, Italy
1959–present

Ralph N. Rosenborg
b. 1913, Brooklyn, New York

Alvin Ross
b. 1920, Vineland, New Jersey
d. 1975
1950–1975

Mark Rothko
b. 1903, Dvinska, U.S.S.R.   d. 1970
1945, 1958–1959, 1968

Judith Rothschild
b. 1922, New York, New York
1949–present

Helen Sawyer
b. 1900, Washington, D.C.
1927, 1954–1972

Nene Schardt
b. 1906, New London, Connecticut
1946–present

JoAnne Schneider
b. 1919, Lima Ohio
1960's

Manfred Schwartz
b. 1909, Lodz, Poland   d. 1970
late 1950's

Therese Schwartz
b. 1927, New York, New York
1948–1966

Jochen Seidel
b. 1924, Bitterfield, Germany   d. 1971
1964

Ben Shahn
b. 1898, Kovno, Lithuania   d. 1969
1925–1935

Judith Shahn
b. 1929, Paris, France
1930–present

Mary Shaier
b. 1905, New York, New York   d. 1971
1949–1971

Jehan Shaly
b. 1928, Detroit, Michigan
1960–1964, 1966

Aaron Shikler
(Information not obtained)

Maurice Sievan
b. 1898, Ukraine, U.S.S.R.
1957–1968

Raymond Simboli
(Information not obtained)

James Simpson
b. 1925, Rotan, Texas
1950–present

Oscar Snow
(Information not obtained)

Raphael Soyer
b. 1899, U.S.S.R.
1928–30, 1954, 1957, 1974–75

Eugene Sparks
(Information not obtained)

Niles Spencer
b. 1893, Pawtucket, Rhode Island
d. 1952
1924–1940

Maud Hunt Squire
b. 1873, Cincinnati, Ohio
1916–1920

Henry Steig
b. 1906, New York, New York   d. 1973
1949–1973

Maurice Sterne
b. 1877, Libau, U.S.S.R.   d. 1957
1915–1947

Pearl Stillman
b. ?
1950's

Myron Stout
b. 1908, Denton, Texas
1938, 1946–present

Sabina Teichman
b.   , New York, New York
1934–present

Rozsi Tevan
b. ?
late 1960's–early 1970's

Bob Thompson
b. 1937, Louisville, Kentucky   d. 1966
1958–1959, 1965

Selina Triefe
b. 1934, Brooklyn, New York
1955, 1961–1963

Jack Tworkov
b. 1900, Biala, Poland
1923–1935, 1954–present

Nadine Valenti
b. 1927, New York, New York
1949–1972

Anton Van Derek
b. 1901, Chicago, Illinois   d. 1943
1928–1943

Frederic Varaday
b. 1908
1951–1962

Anthony Marr Vevers
b. 1926, London, England
1955–present

Ferol Warthem
b.
1930–present

Abraham Walkowitz
b. 1880, Tumen, U.S.S.R.   d. 1965
1916, 1929, 1932

Frederick Judd Waugh
b. 1861, Bordentown, New Jersey
d. 1940
1916–1940

Coulton Waugh
b. 1896, St. Ives, Cornwall, England
d. 1973
1925–1943

Ambrose Webster
b. 1869, Charlestown, Massachusetts
d. 1935
1900–1935

Agnes Weinrich
b. ?, Iowa   d. 1946
1915–1937

Ray Martan Wells
b. 1908, New York, New York
1952–present

John Whorf
b. 1903, Winthrop, Massachusetts
d. 1959
1905–1959

Sol Wilson
b. 1897, Vilmo, Poland   d. 1974
1947–1974

Marjorie Windust
b. 1908, Paris, France
1926–present

Donald Frederick Witherstine
b. 1895, Herkimer, New York   d. 1961
1911–1961

Ben Wolf
b. 1914, Philadelphia, Pennsylvania
1945–1950's

Jan Wunderman
b. 1921, Canada
1959–1969

Taro Yamomoto
b. 1919, Hollywood, California
1951–present

George Yater
b. 1910, Madison, Indiana
1931–present

Arthur Young
b. ?   d. 1943
1929

Marguerite Zorach
b. 1887, Santa Rosa, California
d. 1968
1916, 1920's, 1930's

William Zorach
b. 1887, Eurburg, Lithuania   d. 1966
1914, 1916, 1921

Notes: The dates in this list were taken
from various references; books,
periodicals, museum records, and the
memories of those who knew the
artists. Dates are sometimes
approximated, especially when they
have been obtained from the artists'
acquaintances. It has been impossible
to find data on some of the more
obscure and more unreachable artists.

LENDERS

Museums and Other Institutions and Their Directors

Robert T. Buck, Jr., Albright-Knox Gallery, Buffalo, New York

Richard N. Gregg, Allentown Art Museum, Allentown, Pennsylvania

Leon Anthony Arkus, Carnegie Institute, Museum of Art, Pittsburgh, Pennsylvania.

Mario Amaya, Chrysler Art Museum at Norfolk, Norfolk, Virginia

Josephine Del Deo, Heritage Museum, Provincetown, Massachusetts

Edward H. Dwight, Munson-Williams-Proctor Institute, Utica, New York

Norman A. Geske, University of Nebraska-Lincoln Art Galleries, Lincoln, Nebraska

Ciriazo Cozzi, Provincetown Art Association, Provincetown, Massachusetts

Robert W. Killoran, Town of Provincetown, Provincetown, Massachusetts

Dr. Stephen E. Ostrow, Museum of Art, Rhode Island School of Design, Providence, Rhode Island

Dr. Alfred Collette, Syracuse University Art Collection, Syracuse, New York

Paul C. Mills, Santa Barbara Museum of Art, Santa Barbara, California

Richard E. Oldenburg, Museum of Modern Art, New York, New York

Edward Bryant, Picker Art Gallery, Colgate University, Hamilton, New York

Thomas Armstrong, Whitney Museum of American Art, New York, New York

Edward W. Lipowitz, Canajoharie Library and Art Gallery, Canajoharie, New York

Art Galleries

A.C.A. Gallery, New York, New York

Lee Ault & Co., Inc., New York, New York

Babcock Galleries, New York, New York

Grace Borgenicht Gallery, New York, New York

Chapellier Galleries, Inc., New York, New York

Coe Kerr Gallery, New York, New York

Andre Emmerich Gallery, New York, New York

Forum Gallery, New York, New York

John Gibson Gallery, New York, New York

Gruenebaum Gallery, New York, New York

Nancy Hoffmann Gallery, New York, New York

Martha Jackson Gallery, New York, New York

Landmark Gallery, New York, New York

Kraushaar Galleries, New York, New York

Marlborough Gallery, New York, New York

Milch Galleries, New York, New York

Frank Rehn Gallery, New York, New York

Vose Galleries of Boston, Boston, Massachusetts

Zabriskie Gallery, New York, New York

Private Lenders

Mrs. Courtney Allen, North Truro, Massachusetts

Mr. Benny Andrews, New York, New York

Milton Avery Trust, New York, New York

Mr. Robert Beauchamp, New York, New York

Mr. John Blumberg, Syracuse, New York

Anne Brigadier, New York, New York

Peter Busa, South Hampton, New York

Arthur Cohen, New York, New York

Nassos Daphnis, New York, New York

Mrs. Roselle Davis, Provincetown, Massachusetts

Mrs. Pat DeGroot, Provincetown, Massachusetts

Salvatore Del Deo, Provincetown,
Massachusetts
Mr. William Draper, New York, New
York
Mr. Reeves Euler, Provincetown,
Massachusetts
Mr. & Mrs. Jerry Farnsworth,
Provincetown, Massachusetts
Ms. Perle Fine, The Springs, New York
Mr. William Freed, Provincetown,
Massachusetts
James E. Gahagan, Jr., Plainfield,
Vermont
Mr. & Mrs. Lawrence Gates,
Providence, Rhode Island
Edward Giobbi, Katonah, New York
Mr. Xavier Gonzalez, New York, New
York
Mrs. Adolph Gottlieb, New York, New
York
Mr. & Mrs. Leonard Granoff,
Providence, Rhode Island
John Grillo, Cambridge,
Massachusetts
Mrs. Daniel Hiebert, Provincetown,
Massachusetts
Ruth Hiebert, Provincetown,
Massachusetts
Mr. Henry Hensche, Provincetown,
Massachusetts
Budd Hopkins, Truro, Massachusetts
Mrs. William Hull, State College,
Pennsylvania
Robert D. Hunter, Boston,
Massachusetts
Angelo Ippolito, Binghamton, New York
Mrs. Martha Kantor, New City, New
York
Mr. Joseph Kaplan, Provincetown,
Massachusetts
Alex Katz, New York, New York
Lila Katzen, New York, New York
Yeffe Kimball, New York, New York
Estate of Franz Kline, New York, New
York
Mr. & Mrs. Fred Lerman, Syracuse,
New York
Esther Locke, Provincetown,
Massachusetts
Jason McCoy, New York, New York
Bruce McKain, Provincetown,
Massachusetts
Philip C. Malicoat, Provincetown,
Massachusetts
Blanche Manso, New York, New York

Herman Maril, Baltimore, Maryland
Nancy O. Merrill, Provincetown,
Massachusetts
Robert Miller, New York, New York
Robert Motherwell, Greenwich,
Connecticut
Arnold Newman, New York, New York
Lillian Orlowsky, New York, New York
Mr. & Mrs. Stephen Pace, Washington,
D.C.
Cyril Patrick, Provincetown,
Massachusetts
Lily Pilgrim, New York, New York
Mr. Lawrence Richmond, Great Neck,
New York
Lenore Ross, Provincetown,
Massachusetts
Jo Anne Schneider, New York, New
York
Mrs. Hugo Schwartz, Provincetown,
Massachusetts
Judith Shahn (Dugan), Boulder,
Colorado
Ezra Shahn, Boulder, Colorado
Mr. Edward L. Shein, Providence,
Rhode Island
Mr. James Simpson, Provincetown,
Massachusetts
Raphael Soyer, New York, New York
Sabina Teichman, New York, New York
Mr. & Mrs. Nicholas Wells,
Provincetown, Massachusetts
Mr. & Mrs. Albin H. White, Inglewood
Cliffs, New Jersey
Mr. & Mrs. Howard Wise, New York,
New York
Mr. George Yater, Truro,
Massachusetts
Tessim Zorach, Brooklyn, New York